I Won't Do Wrong

I Won't Do Wrong

Hamish Robertson

authorHOUSE®

AuthorHouse™
1663 Liberty Drive
Bloomington, IN 47403
www.authorhouse.com
Phone: 1-800-839-8640

© 2012 by Hamish Robertson. All rights reserved.

No part of this book may be reproduced, stored in a retrieval system, or transmitted by any means without the written permission of the author.

Published by AuthorHouse 02/27/2012

ISBN: 978-1-4670-0833-4 (sc)
ISBN: 978-1-4670-0834-1 (e)

Any people depicted in stock imagery provided by Thinkstock are models, and such images are being used for illustrative purposes only.
Certain stock imagery © Thinkstock.

This book is printed on acid-free paper.

Because of the dynamic nature of the Internet, any web addresses or links contained in this book may have changed since publication and may no longer be valid. The views expressed in this work are solely those of the author and do not necessarily reflect the views of the publisher, and the publisher hereby disclaims any responsibility for them.

Perplex Forward

I have written this book in order to attain knowledge and wisdom, which has been necessary because of a personal high transient level, which was not self recognised nor believed until years after it should have been. Catch up is not a game to play, but whilst everything must run 'in transience' for accurate analysis, of the environment and of social interaction, I have been exploring possibilities through living and acting in the best way that I can.

So I began to unwind the ball of string that constructs the transient web that so many fall into, and in some cases get stuck for quite a while. I did this until I had measured its length, breadth and width and mapped it out to expose its most dangerous parts. This book represents my journey toward a place where I was within shooting distance of an acceptable vision of its entirety.

I have tried to explore and express as much of the human mind and its links with the universe as I can in order to clarify what to me is 'existence' and the meaning of it. Such research has led me to explain and quantify 'voice hearing', 'non-speak' 'transubstantiation', 'telepathy' and the phenomenon of 'dual dialogue'.

Although I wrote this book to gain a view of life that I see and believe, it has taken a long time compiling data and theories. The lengthy process of proving them takes no more than living a bit longer and waiting for contradiction and affirmation.

I have been on many medicines, and it has taken a long time, but at the age of thirty-four I believe that I have written something worth reading and although not originally set up as a self help book, I hope now that it maybe. It would make me happier for those with mental illness and in particular those suffering from paranoid schizophrenia, to be able to use this book in order to define certain boundaries and draw a line under some delusion. To understand the meaning of an illness, but more importantly to give insight and explanation of paranormal and even supernatural experiences is in my view necessary for any sort of recovery.

Introduction

Mental health has been a recognised part of my life since the age of nineteen when I was first introduced to hospital treatment. Since then I have been set on understanding the realms of the subconscious, of dual realities and of the spirit world (introduced in this book as the Ultra World). I will explore mental illness and in particular psychosis and schizophrenia, which includes voice hearing, hallucinations and delusions.

My theories that put forward explanations of the supernatural and the paranormal, which underline mental illness in this field, are based on real experience. I have suffered greatly and therefore have strived to understand some of the worlds most illusive questions.

I have been as honest and direct as I can, opening as many of the doors into the mind as possible in an attempt to use my life and experience as a case study for my own research. This has been important to me as I am not one who believes for conveniences sake alone. In fact I consider myself to be a man of science, and one who has always wished to share the excitement of the world's treasures with those around me. Because of this and because of the findings I have made, my will to shed light on the workings of God and other vital (in my view) aspects of life has taken me over, and this book been written for my own help. I have fine tuned it for you and anyone else that may be reaching out into a wilderness. I wish to share solace and understanding with God and with the people that I so love and admire.

There is an important fact that must first be learnt in order to get into this book and it is simple. 'Every mind has a propensity for transience. However every mind has a different level of transience but that in God's mind we are all equal.' So there are two ends of the stick one being very strong and noticeable with the power to transcend non speak (read on) which can be called positive transience (transcendental) and the other with a more sheltered level and can be called negative transience or (retranscendental) whose position is ideal for analysis of the workings of the transient mind, because his own is not on show in the same respect. This person ultimately may be very telepathic and yet not able to transcend non speak. Once we have accepted this intrinsic position we can start to look for God.

In order to understand this book from the outset I must explain one or two terms that I have used, the first being 'Non speak.' This is a descriptive phrase that refers to your (native) language through the noise of anything audible (or everything that comes the transient way). For example footsteps, whistling or the judder of a compact drill.(re. ch. 'Whispering sidewalk') The most important non speak converse must come from music, where the notions of non speak are at their most organic. Here we have four minds working on the projection of melody. The musician who is interpreting the structure of the melody that the composer has offered, are one and two. Then there is the conductor and finally the transient; doing his best (Re; chapter 'opt put').

It is important for me to state that the composer creates structure and melody, creating a web or net, and that it is the conductor who directs the non speak. It is evident that the composer is not pinned down by language barriers.

This is also the case of referring bad non speak in your own language abroad where it is not spoken. The non speak in their language will also offer bad transience as God is also talking to them in their language as well. With God working like this an idea of morphic resonance should be considered. (A term used to describe the way notions appear to transcend distance quicker than one would expect). This is also widely unresearched but to believe in God in this way shows the very possible interaction of God's wide reaching arms.

At this point I should explain one of my ideologies that has become the structure of this book. That of 'Destinies Journey' which explains the mental path that one must take in order to find one's place most comfortably in society and the universe.

So I can confirm that being transcendental is having the ability to control non speak, of ones self and others and of any noise coming the transient way. It is a major part of life and an important part of reality that 'destinies journey' would be lost without. And that being retransendental is a position where a mind may stay unheard and unchanging allowing for perfect analysis of the transient world. He can do this as an observer

Along with the notion of non speak control comes the confusion for the voice hearers. In essence the stronger you may be at conducting non speak the higher the chances of being deluded by Ultra life (Re; Chapter voice hearers) as it is with similar ease that one may conduct voices and direct what they say.

Now there are medicines that can help you while you are learning the ways of your transient position in the world and they can help. Many including myself keep on taking them, because you don't mend a broken machine and if your machine isn't broken (with side effects for example) then you are onto a good thing.

Along with 'Destinies journey' I have coined a term 'Best laid path'. There is always a best laid path and it may not always be the easiest. It is the most important thing to remember when you are at your most vulnerable and at these times choosing the best laid path requires strength and consideration. Eventually however your consideration will allow you to follow your 'Best laid path' and once a few of these paths have joined together higher levels of comfort and ease can be attained and consequently maintained and well deserved they are.

Having studied mental health and being a patient in and out of hospital over a number of years (mainly out not in) coupled (among other things)with the idea that I have worked hard hours unloading lorries and that I completed a university fine arts degree I can fairly say that I have had good experience of people no matter the back ground or state of mind and for this I am fortunate as it has increased my confidence so that what I say and suggest has an amount of credibility.

In my early years I bounced off the evidence that no doubt was telling me of my transient position. I was bright, smart and agile and though I had suffered a bang to the head (I'm sure I am not the only baby to be dropped) I can say that it was the protocol that kept me out of links with the world, (Read on), but that once bitten twice shy especially if the wound is not healed the first time. So on a solo mission I began to climb the mountain, needless to say I took a few falls.

However I am happy to say that at this time my life is on an even keel and the doctors and staff have been superb, as I hope I have. I said I will do my best and I believe that is what I have done.

During this time I have completed a degree in Fine Art and have found my painting as important as my writing, in therapeutic and as scientific experiments into unconscious creation of relevant narrative. I had found that this transience in art is largely expressive as 'transient response'. Transient response is something that occurs outside of the conscious mind and is a response to questioning transient input. (Re Chapter Transient response).

Another important theological ideology is the rectification of Decartes 'I think therefore I am' to 'I feel therefore I am,' which allows God more easily into your life.

In addition to previous texts I find it necessary to add a little of my own understanding of spiritual guidance. It is clear that the source of this is everything we understand in ourselves and our surroundings. The muscle twitches for example can create a personal language of converse. In my experience such dialogue can come from three sources; semi-subconscious, subconscious and a larger outside transient force—God/Jungian collective unconscious or even your own unconscious. This is possible while referencing ch.'Voice Hearing' and the idea of a partially separated spirit.

The same can be said about other unexpected noises that may occur (perhaps more to the transcendental) and should be assessed as a matter of obligation, not however acted upon, as everything that is transient has a degree or margin of error.

Before I conclude I would like to introduce the term 'Mentelepathic'. I heard it many years ago whilst talking to an in patient, way before I was ready to analyse its importance and before I could validate any science. However he was referring to a state of general trans telepathy and not as I have done reference half the arena; as my theory states that it is split in two. Which allows for the existence of folly and true physical converse which I refer to as Mentelepathy, but you will have to read the chapter 'Voice Hearing' to understand the characteristics of Mentalepathies related folly.

This book is a collection of works, of actualities, theories, observations, superstitions and tales. I have credited it to be as one as they all represent a faction of my life which has also been my research engine.

Book 1

Actualities

Gone Missing

I had just come back from London and decided that I would still kill myself. I had three pounds twenty to my name. This included a brand new two pound coin that had been minted in celebration of the Commonwealth Games, which had been a total success in the summer of 2002. But I felt no need to benefit from its charm. So with only the clothes I was wearing and the one pound twenty I had left after placing the Commonwealth coin on my side board, I picked up my car keys and headed to the door.

My car was an old BMW 316 a car that I had become quite attached to whilst tinkering about under the bonnet, mending and servicing it. It was to be my chariot for my final journey, of which I knew little about except that it was a conclusion to a nightmarish existence of crazy cross wired thoughts. I had filled up before travelling to London and figured I had enough to get to the car park I was willing to jump from.

Being a person whose thoughts are concerned with people, animals and the transient world, it became clear to me that the skies were beckoning me away from where I had planned to conclude my journey. Reading the clouds was perhaps the only reason why I never made it to the car park.

Having been fully prepared to end myself and being totally in awe of the powers of nature and of the interaction of God in my everyday life, I decided to fulfil a destiny mission and to do this, I was to drive until the petrol ran dry.

I can not remember where I drove but that it was countryside and I was following whichever road that seemed to offer the most escape to the freedom of a promised land. A promised land that every man has the right to journey for.

It was still morning when I came upon the town of Warwick and I turned into St. Nicholas Park. Here I decided to pay for a parking ticket but planned to sit the day out in a most beautiful park. The sun was out and there were three or four park attendants who were busying themselves watering the many flower beds.

Dr. Dolittle had entered my veins and I felt that being guided by the animals would lead me to some success. Magpies have significance to relationships, hence the rhyme 'one for sorrow etc'. This was confusing as the thought I had been aware of when seeing a single Magpie, had been full of the hope and love that came when thinking of a young lady I had fallen in love with. Perhaps they were right, as this relationship was not to flourish and blossom as I had hoped it would.

So here I was in the park with a Magpie eagerly suggesting that I should talk to one of the gardeners. I walked over and introduced myself as a magician. He turned out to be an art student, which at the time I was also. It was all quite well and I wondered for a moment if this young man was the key master. By knowing him could my life turn around, and with that thought a void entered my being. I wished him well and luck in his course and moved on to the river where I could set down and wait for nightfall.

The day seemed to have no end. I sat by the bank of the river and watched the boats glide by to and fro from a small

I Won't Do Wrong

jetty positioned on the other side of a road bridge. It was a perfect day and only my loneliness slowed it down.

There were Canada Geese, Ducks and Swans on the water but it was the Geese that took my attention. It was very strange, they looked at me and then at the water dipping their bills as if to encourage me to take to water. This went on for some time and I was beginning to wonder what they thought would be the benefit for me to be wadding into the water. The thought of walking on water occurred to me and perhaps they were filled with the sincerity that it was possible. They were acting on my thought and maybe in their position . . . . I don't know. I did place my feet on the surface of the water and did experience a strong sensation of firmness, it was however clearly not possible for me to walk here, but I did admire the Geese for their will to help. Maybe to take from the land and to take from the water are two contrasting ways of living and the Geese seemed to be expressing the clear alternative could be to head to the waters (passing thought).

This I contemplated for quite some time. The importance of a dove flying over across the water and a pigeon with white wings set my mind on the crossing. I lay my feet over the side and felt the cool water fill my shoes.

There was a group of children of nine or ten years of age who were playing, they had started to wade into the water, probably because I was, and this was of course not without danger and as one came to me I suggested that they should not wade in the water. Their excitement was more than I could quell but I recommended they enjoyed the sun instead. As they seemed excited by the danger what I said fell on deaf ears. However they were safe, and I was much pleased when a man, with a strong deep voice projected from a passing boat, the words of safety that persuaded them to abandon any river crossing ideas.

My attention was then drawn toward a young couple. They were not far from me but I walked over and introduced myself. I was in telepathy with the young lady who thought she was in telepathy with the young man. God bless them I thought. I crossed my heart and wished them well.

By this time, the day had lasted forever. I weighed up the odds and decided to really run out of petrol. The fuel warning light had been on for some time and although the park was a nice place it was not my space. I was set on finding a better destiny. So I walked to my car, turned the ignition and headed for the exit. It was goodbye to Warwick for the time being.

The journey to my next resting place was and will remain a mysterious labyrinth of corners big roads and small. None the less I ended up near Birmingham.

Interestingly while I was driving I had a genuine belief that, whatever the speed, I could choose a gear that would allow me to run the car on the transient energies and therefore conserve fuel. It went well and I know for sure that I found a motorway. I drove at a steady seventy mph in third gear. My fuel would last longer if I followed this simple rule. Before long I had found somewhere to stop and this is where I decided to leave the car and continue on foot.

By the time I found a place to turn the engine off I was completely lost. I very nearly left the keys in the ignition but a survival instinct, that I still could not shake off, made me lock the car and take the keys. It would be a long time before I would see it again. So I set off on foot, to rediscover a world that I had long since been isolated from, to find a fresh start and a new beginning.

I Won't Do Wrong

I climbed the road and headed down a small lane. It was getting dark by now and within a couple of uneventful miles I noticed mint growing in the hedge row on the last corner before two roads met. The narrow road I was on met a larger more driven route. As I walked round the corner, there appeared an entrance to a small overgrown nature reserve, as noted on a plaque near or on the gate. This is where I spent the night.

This resting place turned out to be a wolf in sheep's clothing. Changing from an ideal place to stay, to the most torturous of places. I remember thinking; 'This is not as perfect as I thought'. But there was nowhere else and here I was. So I figured it was destiny that I should find such a piece of land where I could rest. I looked around and over behind a central tree, as near to the mint as was possible there was a shallow hollow, this I decided would be my sleeping place.

I noticed negative tree forms, (a fallen branch in the shape of the capital letter 'E') and this, with my delusion, knowledge and understanding of shapes, and the metaphoric associations that comprise my world of dual and ultra reality, was not a good sign. There was a crossing of branches that was laid back at forty five degrees, which to me, looked like the apparatus for torture. This was the first part of the conservation area, to the rear of it was the second part. There was only one entrance to this area and there was human faeces in the thinnest part of the joining path (some one must have been caught short). And on walking past this, there was a fly-tipped refrigerator. I decided the first area to be more habitable.

I was picking up on the spiritual side of coincidence and transience. This includes taking notice of shapes and differentiating similar associations. I was picking up bad signs from this 'den', but I had to rest. It was sleep that I feared most. You can not defend yourself whilst asleep. I tried to sleep, I would not fail, I knew that.

What was to happen next will remain with me as one of the worst sensations I allowed myself to endure. As I lay on the ground I vowed not to move until the break of day. This was emotionally one of the most costly and an utterly unnecessary experience, because the transient importance that I was vesting in was folly. However I lay down and got positioned to stay still till the morning. Behind my head, it became apparent, was a stone or piece of wood. I felt, after a short time that my head was open and my brain was spilling out. I found myself paralysed. This was a psychic entity but it was strong. As I lay there I began to notice my visual perception altering, I could see that surrounding me was a perfect white light. Brought down by the gods. However about half way through my resting in what I began to call 'the devils den', I became aware of a foreign body attached to my head. It was a slug (or at least I thought it was. I know now it to have been a leach (probably)). It was desperately trying to get into my head and it was doing this because my brain was spilled out. It seemed to be that it was part of nature and that was its purpose in life. There was no malice though as its non speak was saying 'don't let me in'. But that is exactly what I did. I gave myself this experience. Why? Because I wanted to be as transiently solid and to be as close to God and his will as possible.

So I was there my brain was out and there was a slug entering into my cranium. Anon I finally saw straighter and with a long awaited and abrupt motion I ripped the slug from my head, throwing it some distance away. It felt like half a slug and I wondered if the other half was rattling around in my head somewhere.

I Won't Do Wrong

This experience might have seemed enough for me to leave the den, but it was still late and I managed to get some more rest, if that is what it was, for I did not sleep and barely closed my eyes. It was from this point that I began to hear voices very clearly, and, with holographic accuracy saw people in my peripheral vision. However I still had the apparition of pure white light surrounding me and this gave me a favourable appreciation from God and gave me incredible strength. It is because of this light that I did not acknowledge the holographic apparitions. What I noticed was that to look at a star, (and there were many out) diminished the light around me, and it was this light that was the only thing that kept me from total despair, so I refrained from looking at them, which was a shame because they were out and looking as good as they ever had done.

It was not yet light and on more than one occasion, during this time of rest, I had felt my life to be on a knife edge, in very physical terms, so I decided to leave.

There was a back entrance to the conservation area that I chose to follow. It led into fields and as it was dark and I needed some more rest, I set out to find somewhere peaceful to sleep. On the way there was a transient ally in the form of a cow peering at me with kindness, suggesting the bungalow would help. This was not 'me' I would not burden them and ignored this kindly offer. My idea was of route sixty six, a journey for work and survival. So I left that idea and exited the neglected conservation area, with its two chambers. It had left me disturbed and it was therefore disconcerting to find somewhere similar close by, but once bitten twice shy, so I walked on by. I was much happier in the hedge row of the adjoining field.

Although I did not sleep I was far more relaxed and the non speak of the rats kept me in touch with life. What they were saying I can not remember in detail, but they did ask 'What are you doing?' To which I telepathically answered 'I'm resting'. They were keen to let me know that there was not a problem. This cheered me up and I began to read the clouds, which to me perfectly represented a wizards wand. To be given this gift from the gods boosted my ego and I thought I would plough through the fields in search of that which I was missing, stability, happiness and independence.

As the grass grew longer I became aware that to journey through the fields would be tiresome and almost impossible in the dark, as the hedgerows were impassable and the gates impossible to see. So with some reservation I headed back to the unwelcoming den. It had kept me awake, but the experience was sure to have given me strength. I passed through the den and as I traversed the gate I saw what was to my eyes a porcupine. This, a simple hallucination, was in fact a tuft of grass, however I have had a learned respect for hallucinations and was acquainted with LSD a few years previously.

I shall say that hallucinations can either offer an amused intrigue or a heightened sense of fear. I was matter of fact. I skirted the obstacle and headed the way I had come a few hours previously.

The next forty eight hours would be a real test of physical and mental endurance. Stamina was to play a huge role in my ability to continue. After retracing my steps from the den to the adjoining road only a half mile from my car, I turned right so once again I was headed away from my car and therefore closer to my destiny. I was determined that I should find a life of my own. I was headed toward Birmingham. It is always quite eerie, walking through the most populated places at the still of night. There was the risk

I Won't Do Wrong

of meeting unwelcome situations not to mention encounters with the police and although I was not intent on any crime, I'm sure the authorities would find it in them to sort out my destinies walk for me. In the kindest manner I'm sure, but I was too entranced by my transient senses to be categorised into any institutionalised system. This considered I decided not to go for the city centre, so I headed out of town. After only walking a short distance I came to a path that led me off the main road. I had no idea where I was or where I was headed and that was the part of the experience that kept me going. The path led on for a lot longer than I thought and I grew quite paranoid that it might be someone's private drive way. I came across a large house and as I walked by a security light seemed to be activated. I was a fair distance away and looking down on it so it seemed unaccountable. 'This is not what it looks like.' I could almost see myself saying to the officer in charge. Gladly however the path led on and the imminent immediateness of the situation began to fade away.

The path led onto a main road, after quite some time, whether up onto or down onto I do not recollect. However I was in Aston in the early hours of the morning, walking through the nicer side of town.

Here I saw a sign for hostel accommodation and by this time I was ready to lie in sheets and drift quietly to sleep. I did not find the hostel. Instead I crossed the bridge that passed over the rail line and took up my walk again on the rail line path, which was laid and made good using white chalk stone. This led me to a road at the edge of habitation and I welcomed the freshness of the country air. This road offered one of the strangest experiences I've had. It was a road of cobwebs. As I walked cobwebs enveloped me into claustrophobic anxiety yard after yard, the only way to keep sane was to accept them and wipe my face systematically ever few yards. The road became dark and my feet were hurting from the walk. As I passed under a bridge I looked up and saw a farm barn.

Before, during and after this questful walk I did, and do, have transcendental links with an ultra reality, and the voice hearing aspect of such I call the spirit world. This I have explained later on in the book, but I can rest by saying that at this time I was looking at the barn and I was talking to a friend of mine who offered it up as a place to rest.

I climbed the gate and headed to the barn. I was immediately aware of animals already using it, whether they were horses or cows I will never know, but I did know that they didn't mind me using it. I lay on some straw that had been laid down for the occupants and immediately my shirt was soaked with urine. Still I remained there, as I was too low in energy and the cold had taken to me, due to the lack of insulation which wearing only a shirt gave me (and trousers). I was wearing my blue suede shoes. No one was treading on them but I was in danger of doing that myself. This had been probably the longest day of my life and I was looking forward to the warmth a new day would bring.

Again I failed to sleep and by dawn I was up and on my way down the road. This sort of delivered me into a 'polite' part of town—the town with green in its name.' I went under a bridge and turned right. Here I walked for about an hour and during this time I passed a golf course, and thought, for a nice morning walk, I would follow the path through it. I walked in two circles one after the other, lasting about an hour each until I realised and decided to take a route out of the area. It was down a busy road but what a nice part of the country to live. Still there were no doors of opportunity for me so I left.

I Won't Do Wrong

Before I knew where I was I had entered Redditch, there was a water tower ahead of me and I eyed it up for access and height. This of course would be high enough to end my rambling quest for destiny. However I would have to be swift as it was now well into the morning and it would not take long before I would cause a commotion and that was not what I wanted nor needed. I calmly turned back to the opportunity and firmly locked the door.

Beyond the water tower, just down the sloping road, I saw a small clump of trees. They caught my interest and I went up to investigate. There was a bed, or just a mattress, glue in clear plastic bags which hung down from branches, rope around a tree and scorch marks in the bark about half way up. This horrifying display of what can only be explained as abuse, led me to walk to another town.

This was the longest stage of the walk so far and it felt like I was travelling east through housing developments and onto a main road past the military prison. It was a main road lined with fields, but it was when I past the prison that I found myself with choices at a roundabout. Turning left I found a nature reserve which I entered, but plans to stay only lasted a few moments. I continued on the road and came to 'the town with no name'.

A quiet town of mainly sixties and seventies housing it had the appearance of a modern use of space. Houses were set back leaving open roads and it was centred around a small lake. I found a blackberry bush and began to collect the fruit from the branches. The taste was exquisite and they lifted my spirits.

I sat by the lake and watched a pair of swans gliding in the water. How perfect they were and how stinking I was. The truth about the state of my unkemptness I was in, came to me when envisaging myself with my hair crawling with maggots. This is hard to explain but the dual reality I was experiencing was one of the ultra world. So for example in a mirror I would be clean but due to the transient levels of the ultra world the delusions were real and possibly even visible to some people (not as literal but some where in my ora). Which at the time my sensations that led me to believe this reality couldn't have been more real and it was terrible. I had to do something or I would lose my grip on reality. I was hungry and had a few coins in my pocket. A kindly old man was heading up the road by the lake. He was walking slowly so I asked him in which direction the shop was, he showed me and I was grateful.

So here I was spending the last of my money on toffee and crisps. I ate, but confusion was setting in and with loads of suspicion of what was in the food I discarded and threw what was left in the bin. This was not difficult as it was bin day.

By this time my left hamstring was hurting so I looked in the next patch of wooded land and came out with a walking stick. It was about four foot long and was not ideal but it gave me some support.

Further down the road out of town I came across a main roundabout with an over-pass, and although it was the road I would have liked to take, I thought that walking this road would be never ending and very unforgiving. It was just then I noticed on my left a garage with a workshop beside. I was happy, for the prospect of drinking water and rinsing my hair. I moved over and with permission drank and wetted my face and hair. I felt refreshed and continued on a road that seemed familiar. In fact it was the road that I had passed, with the conservation area to one side. I crossed over and entered into the wooded land to look for a more appropriate stick. And there I saw it 'Excalibur'. It had a handle with three or four shoots protecting the hand, it was a perfect length and tapered into a perfect finish. I believed I had done it I had found Escalibur. It was surely a better stick so I left feeling, at that moment, perfectly contented.

The next road I chose was busy and at some points dual carriage way. I was transfixed with the power that this stick had, and also with the potential of other pieces of rubbish that appeared to have intrinsic importance. Picking them up spontaneously was doing good for a parallel life and increased my transient strength. However with all of this supernatural importance every step was becoming harder to face, I was beginning to feel over burdened with responsibility of being a powerful transient.

Perhaps I had acquired too much magic to be in control of. Down this road I passed a dead fox and a dead dog. They were very close to each other and had been rolled by some sort of verge cutter and were as flat as they could have been, they were road kill. All this seemed evidence of my power in the transient world was out of control which could have been bad not just for me but others. Very soon I entered a town, this again was Redditch I found the local park and spent some enjoyable time basking in the sun. As I carried on through the park, I noticed some people playing football, they must have only been three or four years younger than me and I sat there wondering where my happy days had gone. I left them to play and having been partially cheered up by memory I continued to wonder the park. Here I decided to contemplate 'Excalibur'. I had no right to control such a central piece of magic and in a heart rendering moment I broke it in two and threw the two parts into a small lake that bordered the park, this way I was giving the gift back ready to be found again (in a different form). I was almost asleep on my feet and sat in the sun after dinning on blackberries. I left the park and before long I was passing through a housing estate and noticed a door open. Here I thought were friendly folk. So I rang the doorbell and an astute young man came to the door and obliged my request for a glass of water, the most delicious glass of water I think I am ever likely to taste.

Carrying along the footpath leading out of the estate, I reached an embankment opposite a Tesco superstore and wondered how I could get some nourishment,—a building stacked full of food—Just a chocolate bar, but I soon banished the idea, and followed the path to a nearby underpass and chose to rest on the small grassy verge. Here I lay back and read the clouds. It was starting to rain so I moved on sure that the clouds were in transience with me, and to be honest there is not much more you can do sometimes but be in transience.

I headed out of town along a main road with Worcester sign posted ahead. Fortunately I came across an apple tree and found a full sized apple. The taste was surprisingly bland but I was glad to have found something of substance that was edible. I kept walking, keen that I should visit Worcester. Walking along these roads was verging on J-walking, and my safety, although not strictly in danger was compromised by two lanes of speeding vehicles coming from behind. I came to a roundabout at the edge of Redditch and decided to ask a lorry driver for a lift. He said that this was not possible. On first perception he was honest and discerning, a man of middle age, his cab was clean and he was working to the rule of no hitch hikers I don't blame him I probably didn't smell too good. However there was a phone box just opposite and to my knowledge I had ten pence unspent. I had not used a public phone box for quite some time and to my dismay the minimum tariff had been extended to twenty pence. Reversing calls could have been an option but I was determined to climb out of the hole I was in and to reverse call was too intransient. Clearly though I hoped this hole to be a tunnel, the difference being the light at the end. So I was left once again with the choice of Worcester or the romantic Shakespearian town of Stratford. I was seduced by this romance and before long I had crossed into the county of Warwickshire. On crossing the border, I wondered into a field. The gates were open and fresh ploughed soil led me in and I picked up two or three stones. As a transient I could read stones and I was careful which ones I chose.

By dusk I had journeyed only a few miles and felt it time to leave the main road and when I came across a sign for 'a town with lee in its name', I veered off and entered a road bordered with trees.

The darkness had enveloped me and my hallucinations became very strong. This road must have been only two or three miles and at its end were two pubs. The one on the right was playing loud music, this I enjoyed, but with no money I had to walk on. The night life in this small town was warm and sparkling, a good time being had by all. I headed out to find somewhere as warm as I could.

Firstly I tried a field and the walking northwards, I came to a T-junction with Birmingham signed to the right. There was an embankment and as I approached a tree at the top of this raised land I was wary not to disturb anyone already asleep there. The coast was clear, but I still had bad feelings for this place. My hallucinations were sinister under this tree, and the street lamp adjacent to it was dim red colour, not as the others which were orange. After correlating these thoughts I decided to move back into the small town that I had just left. I walked to the centre of town and took a left down a hill and eventually, out into the countryside. Here I had two choices, one was a grave yard and the other a field. I walked to and fro between them until I realised that the grave yard was not a grave yard at all. I decided to sleep there as it was more sheltered from the elements than the field; a basic choice, survival instinct, for I knew the powers of the cold and I was now quite undernourished. However it did help to know that it was not a field for burying the dead. The house opposite was supporting a security light, the ground was crunching with loose gravel so with feather feet I headed back toward the field, this place was too open after all.

So I headed to the other site, there was a lay-by and a style there. I climbed it and headed to the flattest part. In fact I was laying on what remained of a pile of straw and dung, I thought how can this happen two nights in a row, was there a radar out for me to find them? Never mind I was so cold though and this appeared to be the best place to lie. This was the most sheltered place and as I was only wearing a shirt and trousers my core body temperature was at a knife edge, which of course is called hypothermia which can be fatal. I stayed there for an hour or two, during which time only one car stopped, its lights flashed through the hedge that I was directly behind. I heard the muffled voices and as quickly as they had come they left.

I got up again and now I was limping quite distinctly. After seeing where this road led to, and after deciding to try a footpath that proved impossible without local knowledge, I ended up back in the town with Lee in its name', where I saw the final quest for my destiny on a sign post promoting Evesham. This road was very long and very straight and although I felt Evesham would be intrinsically strenuous, I figured it was the only true path for me to take.

I Won't Do Wrong

About an hour and a half into my Evesham walk I came across a lone house. A light was on and I stepped quietly to pass unnoticed. As I was alongside it I heard a rustle in the garden foliage. Here I was in a moral dilemma, should I investigate or leave alone? I was not sure of the time but it had been dark for a few hours. I kept my ears open, it was life of that I was sure, whether human or not I could not say. There were no cars in the proximity, so if it were an assailant he would have had to have been on a midnight walk as I was, and that seemed unlikely. So with new fear that it was the occupant of the house collecting wood I moved on. with hindsight I suspect it to have been a fox, one thing was sure we both noticed each other.

I suppose another hour had passed when I came across a mansion. It was built of stone and set back from the road. The moon must have been out as it was illuminated against a dark background and waves of mist, that hung in the air, shrouded it with mystery and romance.

As dawn broke I had made good headway and I soon came to a turning. I took this turning under a bridge and up the hill the other side. I was still in an obsessive mood of transient responsibility and had decided that I should not walk past a white feather. However after much deliberation and no real hope of being able to fulfil this desire, I decided to accept this burden and picked one up and placed it in my pocket with my other finds.

Soon I was walking in the country, with an old house on my right and a farm lane on my left. The house on my right I believe to have been an ex psychiatric retreat, which seemed kind of apt. The farm however could offer me work, but because of the state I was in, I declined my offer of attempting to earn money. Perhaps I should have taken that path and maybe I could have earned my keep, or perhaps I could have been turned away, I shall never know.

The next road was the road of falling acorns. I had never experienced such a shower of acorns. Needless to say I picked up an acorn to keep my energy good. I would have liked to have slept in the ditch. I found a good place where the hedge was split leaving a small dugout. Climbing in I saw a shotgun cartridge and realised that in any case it was too cold to lie down on the wet ground.

It turned into a fine day and the sun shone down and was a needed escape from the cold. Here I walked along a road leading to some sort of habitation. I found a white cord, which I differentiated as a transient warning of being kidnapped and even hung. I was wary of every van that drove by. The habitation I had seen to the top of the hill turned out to be only a small number of houses lining the road, but before I reached them I discovered a small warehouse or garage. After finding the cord I had felt bad energy from this place, but whatever fate I had waiting for me, I wished to conclude for better or worse. I could have walked on but the lack of knowledge would have weakened me as I would not have been facing my anxieties . . . Thankfully there was no one there. I was glad that I was wrong.

I headed down the road until I came to a big roundabout. I found my way onto a dual carriage way and walked for most of the day. Eventually I came to a position where the road over flew another; this was the turning to Evesham.

I had developed a serious limp and my body was aching in all sorts of directions. And I was again faced with the choice of Sratford-on-Avon or Evesham. The road to Evesham was a much darker road than the one to Stratford, but I felt that my luck was out and of all the destinations I had ahead of me. I decided that this was the place where

I Won't Do Wrong

I would stop walking and take of my shoes, it would be Evesham.

This road I stayed on all night with lorries and cars passing somewhat infrequently but consistently in both directions. It was a newly built road with two lanes in both directions, the side-walk was tough going, as it was constructed for drainage purposes and not for walking. The construction of this road had not included the setting of lights, so not only was it loud and hard to walk, it was dark as well. I started reading the clouds and even thought that the road was being used by the same lorries that would pass, turn round, and drive by again. I figured the last place that anyone went to was Evesham, to be incarcerated, medicated and never let go. So I was making a huge decision in continuing this road and I decided that the more the lorries went one way (out of Evesham) the more I was being guided back to the happiness and security that I had once known. Calculation that I was on a knife edge I began to read the clouds. I can't remember what I saw it was all to spontaneous and rapidly changing, but there was some terrible pain and indecision including torture. However I was saved by the compassion and strength of the spirits of friends that guided me back. Back to the junction I had been a night time ago, between Stratford and Evesham. There was a travel lodge and a Burger King and I guessed that this complex was set up for those contemplating this most treacherous of journeys. So I walked up to the door thinking that I had beaten the negative side of transience and had been allowed to live. I expected warm water and clean towels. However I was ignored, just another tramp wanting something for nothing. A car pulled up into the car park, my spirits were raised by this man. I had hope for the lend of a phone call. I asked for ten pence and he obliged.

I had spent the other ten pence and left realising that this would not be enough, but I seemed to withdraw from the help another ten pence could offer so I did not ask.

I set off on the way to Stratford, my head was saying that this was the best way. However the ultra world was battling with my judgement. I knew I was right but my quest for a place to stay was offering the different route. Not to Evesham but back nearer to where I lived. I knew the right road was that to Stratford but for love and respect to the spirit that offered me an escape from hell I was compelled to accept this advice. For the five minutes that I was undecided, I experienced a strange sensation in my head. The maggots were back and I must have counted forty or fifty entering my brain (I could feel them both leaving and entering - at this point they were entering). My whole being was saying Stratford now and I set off in that direction. The sun was out and I continued down yet another dangerous road with lorries passing me, sometimes less than one or two feet away. I was walking on the left hand side of the road where I came upon a lay-by. I was in more of a mess than I had never been before, my mind was swirling with tiredness and as I closed my eyes I briefly wondered whether they would open again. I had drained myself of the ability to converse with the outside world. I sat down I was over wrought with failure, my mind was tired but I knew that to sleep might be final.

So I stood up, and wondered down the road, which was on a downward slope I thought that I would rather walk than to lie down and with my soul saying 'don't lie down and let evil triumph' I was stronger than that.

The road had a downward gradient I saw a sign for a small village. Public phone box I decided. Walking was becoming more difficult as my left knee was seizing. I made

I Won't Do Wrong

it through and found the village to be up a smaller hill and this is where I imagined the phone to be. There was no phone box, so I chose a house from the village to help with my direction home.

Although they were at first keen to help me, they gradually captured the stench of my clothes; and took in my dishevelled appearance. The unshaven beard which was hiding an infection that I hadn't noticed, the state of my clothes and the vagueness of my tired mind. He put the phone down and suggested that the lorries parked at the top of the hill would be my best bet. I am not sure if it was the ultra world that prevented him from helping my guess is that it was. So with more than a little disappointment I began to climb the hill. One after another the lorries turned me down so I walked halfway back down the hill to the lay-by I had previously found. Here there was a Volks Wagon campervan I headed across and the driver a young man in his late teens early twenties chose to ignore me and an older man who I guessed to be his father opened a curtain from the back and told me there was no room for free-loaders.

However my luck was about to change, a man pulled up in a four by four trailer back. He looked as if to be surveying the lay-by and I thought to ask if I could catch a lift to Stratford.

After phoning through he agreed and it was on his way so I got in and set about talking, after all he was a very welcome turn up for me. I thought I was ok but clearly I was not. He suggested that I should check in to the mental health clinic at Stratford hospital. And I said that I probably would, but I would not go there just yet.

So after wandering Stratford for half the day I decided to take the good mans advice and went to find the hospital. The roads on which I came I tried to retrace but there was no sight of the hospital, and when deciding how hard I should look I noticed two men loading a car. I asked them for directions and they could do one better and drive me there as they were ready to leave. Finally I figured that my journey had finished. I opened the door to the hospital clinic and was seen by a doctor in not much time. As he sat he touched the wood of the table and started to speak.

The curious twist to the story is that I was driven to St Michael's hospital in Warwick, which was close to St Nicholas's park where I had first stopped my car to consider my destiny.

The question I wonder, was I trying to defeat destiny or was I looking for it. The romantic in me cries that the journeys of the heart are what makes our world unite and they should never be discarded. And that just if sometimes they make complete circuits this does not mean that the journey is therefore void of purpose. Far from it, such journeys whether physical or spiritual can give enlightenment and a sense of doing all you can and give an understanding of what should remain important in life, that being love . . .

Whispering Sidewalk

This chapter relates to a single journey where the path of non speak shows the cognitive relevance of thought. The faith and skill involved is and should be learnt as a part of the process of growing up. It does however show as new to a transcendental who may have been 'lock out' at the early stages of discovery and who consequently has been hitching a ride with God oblivious to mainstream theodicy. Therefore to some it will sound a little obvious and perhaps even prudish. The position that I am in is somewhat different to most but the basic idea is relevant to all.

It started with the noise of the front door and the footsteps of myself. 'Oh that's a horse clip clopping by'. There it is my focus, an introduction to non speak.

Now the door is closing and then walking to the driver side of my car. 'I admire the non speak' pronounces the non speak. 'Your nearly there' speaks the starter. 'O.K.' I say as I engage reverse. I looked over my shoulder and heard a pigeon singing; 'You deserve her, you deserve her.' That's good. 'Don't give in' speaks the tyre crunching through the gravel of the drive way.

'Thank you' I say and gesture as someone waits for me to leave the gate, I'm not quite sure what I said there I'm a good man and God will have represented me well.

It's a fair drive to town and I let myself concern about the radio. Does a tree make a noise if no one is near enough to hear it? Yes is my preference of answer but only in the respect that the tree falling is connected via the ultra world to respondent(s). So it may, but also it may not. In fact I've only heard one tree fall and I was surprised to wake up the next day, for I heard it at night, to find that it was not my neighbours tree, it was no ones tree but it was a tree wasn't it?

Here we are, the superstore car park, bit of a walk but it's free. 'Oh sorry I say as my door nearly clashes, 'Lovely person' I request my non speak. There is noise around and it is time for me to decide what rhythm of transient noise I should surf and adapt.

Yes be learned and wise but try not to solve everyone's troubles, firstly its too hard and secondly they're just getting around just like you. But hold a door open chivalry is not dead.

Rattle rattle rattle carves a spiralling trolley wheel through the audible world. Fear not if there are two sides of a coin they may both be shown. By which I mean that noise need not be always be talking (non speak), tumble weed and the noises of silence and of God complete audible interaction. Treasure them and think: 'I know it's not my world but Gods and everyone else's as well.'

'I hope that you marry, Yes she's fantastic.' grate the trolley wheels as the world wakes up and starts to converse: 'Don't give in don't give in'. This is all good but I don't want to keep the line open. It's not as simple as hanging up the phone. No the perfect scenario is for a smooth transition between transient sources. How is this done? Well you have to think about what is important to you whether it be tranquillity, intellectual philosophy, comedy, chivalry, eccentricity or something else but faith in mankind is probably the best answer.

So with the aim for my transcendental strength to be put to most use I like to self educate in order to learn my

I Won't Do Wrong

strengths and weaknesses so that I am constantly learning and improving, 'you only live once so don't never let it go'.

I see a mother walking with her two children. She smiled and so I directed non speak: 'God willing that I may be a father one day.' and looked up into the sky.

That's a good point where was that shop? 'Don't give in, don't give in'

"After you." I say holding the door.

"Thank you."

"Pleasure." I say wondering why the world can not always be so at rest.

My word I hadn't heard the till. 'No idea', I know it was good but I was snipping at the last bit and such a thing can turn anything upside down and shows the importance of faith. 'You deserve her.' The till projected. That was good, I didn't even hear it I thought as I walked over to the men's clothing.

Red chequered shirt. 'Is it nice?' I thought 'A bit like a lumberjack and that's pretty cool. Exploration with colour, cut etc'. I remembered thinking 'I will buy that.' I put it back on the shelf. 'Just do the rounds.' I thought.

'I think you should' I heard as I left the shop. It will be O.K. it will be O.K. drives my non speak. Here's the shop with my wizard's companions (referencing an ornament that I had bought). The version of my wizard was not there but others in the series were. I like the one holding the purple glass heart. May be one Christmas or birthday. "Just go to one shop, the Red Cross" I thought to myself. "Its not far, right next door to the coffee shop I think."

So I headed down the road and just before the Red Cross (my next charity shop) is the coffee shop so I stopped for a coffee.

It was market day and there were all manner of stalls, of the type found in a small town. I always find such places intriguing basic trade; you want; you buy; you move on: great stuff.

Before long we entered the shop I felt very penned in and with nothing that I wanted I was about to leave.

'Your right your right', I hear the non speak of a man who entered at the same time as me and who left at the same time. This is all fine and the more occupied you are the less important cohering to transient response is, as gradually the need and ability leaves you and that's good as well.

So I got my coffee and sat outside at a table that had been set up for the fine day that it was.

A lady walked past with clip clopy shoe's that I noticed out of all the noise. This is an example where to 'opt out' (Re chapter) would have been wrong and whilst trying to talk to the waitress I sensed it necessary to direct her non speak. It is always harder to direct non speak of living respondents rather than 'external noise' such as the sound of a bus going by, simply because there is no extra dependent save God. Where as conscious life demands a little more thought. This is partly because God is more forgiving but also because you have a relationship with God and not necessarily with someone whom is just walking past you.

A scenario that occurs once in a while is to forget what you mean or what to say (in non speak) because this encroaches on the spontaneity of converse. Some people will save you some of the time, but you must concentrate on what it is you want to think, which doesn't even have to be the same topic just what you want to say.

'I do my best, don't give in, I'm made up for you', I direct her non speak in bars of three.

I Won't Do Wrong

"Just get some cash out" I thought glancing over at the cash machine opposite. I weave between the market stalls and find myself waiting in a queue. Bread and butter stuff. 'Don't give in' I request the noise of her pin number. I started to stare into space and noticed her child was doing the same, I looked at him and looked around and then directed the non speak to say; 'just waiting to get some money.'

It was late in the shopping day now and I was pleased to let the town go about its business and allowed myself to drift into a day dream and trance whilst walking back up the market hill. I look in one more shop, bought a fleece for a fiver and then onto my last stop to get my shirt. My shopping day complete I said good bye to the town and headed off home.

I feel that this response to ones surroundings shows the rudiment of transient co-existence, it is therefore your own responsibility to act in as good a way as befits your manner. It will get easier the longer you live and should become automatic and 99% of the time easy with the other 1% intellectually managed. Well we are not machines, no it is about faith and you can't just decide to have mastered faith instead it comes with the results of being good and straight and brave and kind.

Four Seasons

It was the fourteenth of February 2000 and Peter was celebrating his birthday. Being a valentine boy had not bought him the kind of luck he had expected over the years. Aged 29 unlucky in love and getting older by the day he had resided himself to being his own rock. He found that friends were easy to keep, but he was suspicious of what they expected and more so of what they were taking. He was pleased enough with the idea that he could be friendly to anyone and therefore anyone and most people would be friendly to him. All the rest seemed like a woeful waste of his religious time.

With the post that arrived late morning Pete found to his surprise a card coloured pink and that smelled of perfumed. His heart rate increased just slightly, this he thought must be some sort of joke. He was in expectant until his mind wondered to whom it was from and there was a twinkle in his eye as he envisioned Dannie from work.

Pete worked for the Royal Mail in a Ulesthorpe sorting office and had often caught something in the gaze and smile of Dannie whose day to day conversations were very precious to him. He had known her for all of the three years that he had worked there, and with this card he realised that he loved her. He was not sure if the card was from her or even whether she knew he had these feelings for her, but he opened it with hope all the same.

I Won't Do Wrong

While he thought he had no close friends everyone did like him, it was the fact that he was very transcendental which set him apart. The stand point from most people who new him mimicked the fact that he was clearly blind to his individuality. A precise personality he had, he was one that could not hide a thing, and what he said was always interesting but others clearly saw more than he did on what he was saying. His needs were attractive but it was a sort of one way situation and he had learnt that to get more he should give less.

Nothing however passed the notice of his friend Duncan who could read him like a book, and whom Pete admired very much.

'Yes, it is Valentines day.' She smiled and handed him a card.

'But you've already . . . I never got you one.'

At which point she said 'Its your birthday stupid.' Then he saw the card propped up on her desk, he picked it up and it read; 'To my dearest Dannie love love and love from Mark.'

It was now that the train ran over him.

'Arrr.' He said 'He is a lucky man.'

'He might not be.' Whispered Dannie.

By which time Pete's mind had left the building and the last emphasis had gone right over his head and in a sort of retreat he touched the wooden desk and walked away.

The truth was that he didn't know what to say. He hated saying the wrong thing, that was his woe, so sometimes when he really ought to speak he did not. He was not one for half hearted analysis and was often not in the right mindset for analytical judgement so all to often he didn't try. He especially felt this in the affairs of the heart, despite the lack of spontaneity that implied. But he felt he needed to know how hard the ground was and once he knew that he was fine. Problem was by that time the chance had usually gone.

So he had to sit and think, to re-workout the sideways glances and the body language, the time their hands touched in the canteen, and the way she looked and smiled. He knew all this already, but was his interpretation of their relationship as colleagues and friends accurate, now that she has a boyfriend?

'He might not be.' Pete kept repeating. 'That means I might be! So should I be flattered? Of course' He thought. And with that he sat at his desk and smiled and glancing across to Suzie who looked back at him before carrying on with what she was doing.

But the card this morning, this surely couldn't explain. Unless . . . He looked across to the two young lads that were always stirring for their own amusement. They had only been working there for six months and still had a schoolish and slightly obtuse sense of humour, the type that surrounds those used to the safety and confinement of institutional status quo. Somewhere that only intellect prevails and where a real understanding of the consequences of anxiety and stability hold. A small wonder, where existence is somewhat smothered by the immortal process of being young. With a real sense of the ego and its powers and without a real implication of cause and effect.

Their names were Dave and Paul, and Pete looked across, as the penny dropped, in a far from angry way and wondered what on earth was his life worth. The butt of practical jokes an insane lack of success with the girls and his obsession with Dannie who in the law of poetry he was destined to be with.

I Won't Do Wrong

'They been playing up again?' Asked Duncan. 'They sent the card.'

'Is there anything you don't know about me?' Pete stammered.

'Come on mate it's me remember.'

'I sometimes wonder if I'm the last to know my own business.'

'The stuff you miss or pass by it's incredible, you believe everything that you are told.'

'That's not exactly fair.' Said Pete in his defence.

'Ok some people can say anything and you can't work it out, because you are truthful doesn't mean that others are. The fact is that you have an extreme life experience for someone your age and others wonder why you can be so worldly you have a justified answer to everything, doesn't mean everyone does. Do you see where I'm going?

'I think so isn't that just my memory and the way I remember stuff? Photographically?'

'That's what I mean, you are probably the most intelligent person in here but when it comes to the psychology of social interaction: Its like your intelligence is turned off, like you want the world to be perfect and people pick up on that and start saying things. Things that would fit perfectly but only because it's what you want hear, which is the truth, you accept it as just that. Now go over and ask Dannie out, and if she says no then leave it there. You know you are creative yes?'

'Yes.'

'Well that makes it harder for you to believe something that you do not wish to hear. Simply because it is what you want and you use your intelligence to verify what you want to believe, and it can become hard for some to try and say, that she will open the door to your kindness which of course you will misinterpret and I'm afraid this kind of cycle becomes hard to break, and that my friend is a dead end street.'

'Bloody hell Dunc . . . 'Said Pete. At which point the area manager entered the building; Duncan moved on and productivity increased slightly.

Chapter 2

What Duncan had told him on that day was probably the single most important piece of psycho analysis that had ever been expressed toward him. And by jove, the gods were willing and Dannie had not said no, so they started dating, starting with that very night after work.

They had arranged to meet at her parents house where she was living.

'Hello, hello. Peter I presume.' Welcomed her mother as she opened the door. Pete was quite surprised as he was not sure of the ex's situation. Would he measure up. A bolt out of the blue should I say, or was it, he was not sure, but either way he was here taking his perfect girl out to town.

He would have liked to have taken her for a meal but they had known each other for over three years and a meal seemed a bit quiet. They both needed fun and maybe a bit of a drunkard kiss. This is what they both knew of each other, honest and hard working. If they were the foundations of something then they were good ones, but if they were to make anything from this then they would have to do more. If they could somehow fulfil ambition as well then surely this was a romance that should be nurtured.

On the late shift at work Dannie, Pete and Duncan and Kate (Duncan's wife, who would join us when she could make it), went to the towns night club to celebrate the start of the weekend. Of course the long slog of the week is worth finishing with a drink. Kate the sweetest level headed young woman was a mother of two youngsters and so the end of the week was not free for her. This is a woman Pete admired very much and his opinion of Duncan was the same, for they were true working class hero's which as John Lennon has told us is something to be.

On one such evening Duncan became profound, this was not unlike him as Pete knew very well. He simply said 'Do something'

To which Pete replied instantaneously 'University?'

'Why not? You can do . . . no you need to do something! If there's one thing that riles me it is the waste of potential. Of intellect lain dormant, if you don't do something you will slowly drown and I won't let you do that. Six months or more of work and you'll be at the next academic year. Apply now or you will drown. There it is, there is something different about you, everyone can see it. If you don't break out of this groove then this cycle of life will bore you and you will drown, it will turn against you and wrap you in its web and stifle your progress. Stay as long as you need but working class hero well that's my badge ~ right.' They both began to laugh and Pete feeling very humbled and optimistic answered simply.

'Yes I will do that.'

'You're to be either an unsung hero or filthy rich, I can't decide. Either way you will learn who you are and your position, because at the moment I'm not sure you know either. It is your responsibility to be who you can be, in a transient way, otherwise the world will never have known you the way you should be known, and to me that's the responsibility of every individual. How otherwise will we be able to fulfil Gods prophecy. It is evolution of the most basic and fundamental nature.'

I Won't Do Wrong

'Your right I know you are and I will do this and I am a man of my word'

The road was to be harder than Duncan had let on, after all it was not up to him to say how possibly terminal this dive into the darkness could be. He was fulfilling his role as a friend to push him for his own good but whether he would fly or not was out of his hands, secretly though he knew.

After this discussion Pete immediately sorted out a place at his local university to which he was unconditionally invited and he walked in with a spring in his step and oodles of commitment and easily enough confidence. He was older than the average student but the mix was good.

He had been to university before in Leeds immediately after finishing school and found a way of life that was too good. Constantly fishing, not for people (of whom he loved) but more for the 'dopy dream' which was cloaking the country with the introduction of the ecstasy tablet. A dream of hallucination and ecstasy. A dream that should have curtailed, but did not, the only things that curtailed were his schooling in engineering and his sanity.

The fact that he was never convinced he was on the right course led to a complacency that led only one way. The way out of university.

It took him a long time to completely say no to a joint or half an ecstasy tab but he did and he did this categorically at twenty seven years old, seven years ago. It was out of necessity that led him free. His mental health deteriorate and he found the paranoia too much to want to handle, let alone if he might be able to. No this was a dead end street. A street that some may want to rent a room on for a while but to buy a house, not for Pete, he knew that (though the idea seemed very attractive to start with). To be honest he bought the t shirt but was now cutting it up to throw away.

But here he was seven years down the line, he has had a job for the past three years, he had a beautiful girlfriend and had been offered a place at university. Life couldn't be going better.

Pete had always had a keen interest in art and had decided—'forget the money the big house and the fast car, I know my vocation; I . . . am an Artist.' He said in a Eureka moment it was a sort of epiphany for him that made him feel somewhat complete.

It was now up to him to ask Dannie if they could move in together. What she knew about the Art course, was that there would be much less money coming in, but she was up for it so she applied for a transfer to his university town, she and he could just about get through on a financial level. The rest was floating in the wind.

So they moved in together to a small flat above a shop, it was cramped and there was no garden or balcony but they would make do at least for the time being.

Chapter 3

He remembered his first chance at university where, faced with a blank canvas, he started to paint a new picture of his life. It was after the new year had started that Pete turned to a time in his life where he was at a social high and where he had the experience of the effects of drugs and dance, a place that no other aspect of life, that he knew of, could compare. The lows he never talked about and his behaviour at the time was in some instance wrong. A naive fool who clearly showed no interest in progression toward adulthood. Finally of course he was to end up undergoing years of treatment in order for him to understand who he was and what he was about.

All this was eleven years ago, but he was able now to sit back and reflect with sobriety on his first try at Uni. He was not going to make the same mistakes again. An excellent time to train as an artist.

With most of his undeniably triptastic experiences being on various designer drugs Pete thought this an ideal place to start. How to define hallucinations of euphoria on canvas with paint?

He was always an optimist and tried to deny some really bad emotions, emotion from his mental illness. He did not understand them but in the end he would have to, simply to understand life in general. And things got worse when Dannie with all her charm left him, whether it was the claustrophobic flat or just a tiredness that was slow to accumulate, showing its head as depression, well the burden became too much, and he did not know how to change, but she did and she left leaving a gapping big hole in his life.

She had left him offering the only thing she could and that was her utmost admiration, and she hoped that that would be enough, she prayed that is was.

Pete thought of what to do. He will paint and paint until once more he could see the light of salvation. His technique had changed through his wild marks on the canvas he began to realise that he was never one hundred percent responsible for the flow of narrative figuration. This was like a gift from the gods. He had something now to get his teeth into, to absorb himself from his otherwise miserable world.

It was about this time that he found God, with reading of contemporary literature he was beginning to arm himself with substantial backing and spiritual guidance.

With work in practice being experimentation of automatism, that no one before him seemed to have done so what he was doing was new in every respect. Painter Jackson Pollock did similarly except he never celebrated the figural accident. Which was the whole concept and magic that had enticed Pete. Where was this figural coming from? Yes he had something really interesting to experiment with. Maybe this is what Duncan was talking about. Perhaps this was who he was. Whatever it was, it took him onto a new level as he tried to prove the authenticity of its abstract construction.

This work was not without its boundaries and it took him more than the allotted time that a degree was offering to fully understand but he would continue none the less. As with most things 'they get worse before they get better' and this was certainly the case in Pete's view. He often presented work that was unfinished by putting too much affirmation on the abstract marks that were the foundation of his narrative. Were they offered to him from a higher source? He was sure that they were though he did realise that this arena included his own unconscious as well all manner of other possibilities including God or a collective unconscious. He knew one thing; it was not a product of his own conscious.

What he did realise, after a time, was that the buck stopped with him, and with it came responsibility. These were offerings but certainly not written in stone.

At about this time Peter began to develop symptoms of the psychosis that he thought he had left behind. It had a new label now and he had to try to manage his life with schizophrenia as well as his extraordinary transcendence and in his opinion, (which he had little choice but to take on) a cutting edge avant-garde artist, which sounded good and gave him hope. Some of his delusions were so terrible and real to him that he began having to live a double life simply to survive. He knew that he must be a good soul and not express his distaste while he believed that he was being abused so. It was for him quite simply hell on earth and with his soul being ripped apart day and night he was crying out for death to embrace him. Forced under the almighty sword of silent authority to take medication, some which could not have been designed to cause worse breath, and being victim of the night monkeys, he in the end relented and tried to take his own life. And though he failed he came very close but just something kept him alive. It seemed as though a dagger had been pushed into his side, one that no one else could see. His manageable life disappeared and acting every day life became impossible.

Before leaving the course he had to take some time off to try and sort stuff out. But he couldn't sort and so relented not expecting to complete. It was not long before he was back in hospital. Fortunately he had been persuaded to ask the university for a sabbatical year, and he was glad that he did because finishing the course was to be, for him, an exceptional performance.

Finish he did, and after much tribulation and strain he was pleased for the experience to be dealt with properly (start here and finish there) a quantum of work and a result of completion. His passion was painting and he tried his best to give it the dedication and attention that it deserved. He was however only able to give his judgement and say what he saw, I don't think he was believed and he had not enough time to prove anything. But like he said at the start he was here for painting not examining. His buzz was to find something in his painting that he had not seen before and that which made him laugh was good.

He was still at the stage where everything that was offered was too trusted, after all it is the artist that must stay responsible for his work and therefore must be happy with its proclamations. A simple error but one that has to be recognised, you are after all only a medium for the unconscious arena and therefore liable to error. But liable for truth as well. It is up to the artist to sort one from the other.

It was with this importance that he strove to justify his apparent ability to dip into the unconscious arena and be able to conduct and assemble its content into honest representation. His theory started with the idea of a collective unconscious that the Jung's theory suggests.

He had worked hard now and though his life was still in a shamble his optimism was good. His hope as he saw it was for success to start (and it just had done) and from very small success, if maintained, could be added too until

I Won't Do Wrong

more and more successes accumulate and at some point if the success is not broken then the theory is you reach the promised land, or at least a point near to it.

It was laid down before him that to be successful one must educate the mind by reading. Pete chose authors such as John Steinbeck, George Orwell along with more modern authors such as Sebastian Faulks who's book 'Human Traces' was most inspiring.

He had also painted to promote the important work of Fair Trade, where a decent wage is contractual to their business. It was a time in the late 1990's where up until the beginning of the Iraq war, there was a sharp interest among the hopeful to affront corporate power by social revolution for the abolition of so called sweat shops, being used by leading brands for maximum profit / minimum wage. It was a time of change but the war ended that. As it would and will turn out globalisation making the world smaller allows for fewer scams, but that does not defer the dampening effect on world esteem that the war has had. Such books like 'No Logo' by Naiomi were best sellers and anti globalisation protests were common place. Though these anti globalisation affair's were not particularly an issue to him, not as Fair Trade was. If anything he preferred the idea of united economies where there may be fewer blind spots for sweat shops with bad health and safety and poor wages etc. to hide.

This of course all stopped when Tony Blair announced that we were at war with Iraq with claims such as their ability to launch a warhead of mass destruction in forty-five minutes.

It was a close call to have to make, but we are a democracy and at the end of the day a million people attended the anti-war march which conveyed popular opinion. However the audience is sometimes wrong and it was far from a nice regime, some heinous crimes were committed and genocide anywhere is unacceptable. And there were acts of genocide although not sustained campaigns. What was sure though was that the war in Afghanistan was necessary for the defence of the western allies, we will find out about Iraq, it is a key stone and I have every confidence in our political work and good values (which to us British is as important as being a good fighter).

What he was sure of was that money was going in the wrong direction but such is the affliction of war. If only we could be left to distribute our success to those who need it. We must prioritise but to be of help firstly you need to be comfortable and safe with your own affairs. So the evil workings of terrorist cells of al'-Qaeda clearly needed sorting before the realisation of a United World showing positive existence can be practiced.

Pete truly believed that when the turmoil of the African countries could be settled and the yin and yan of seasonal work allowed to develop without the threat of warlords taking their cuts, Africa would once again be somewhere peaceful and the most amazing place on Earth to be cherished. And when tribal warfare, which in some places namely the Sudan and Chad borders (the Delfur region) and The Congo, and Somalia together amount to a largely unknown situation much bigger than any would realise. Where the devastation is huge with the destruction being said as 'only seen before on the fields of the Somme'. This might sound surprising because it is. Africa is vast and we see only briefly what hit's the news, and that includes the good things as well. Compassion is clearly an achievable goal and if we had our time freed up we could focus on such issues. We must not forget how we have struggled to win our free secular society and we can not underestimate the difficulties ahead for those who strive to do the same. We are a country with vast experience and a strong arm, a country of wealth in every sense of fundamental living and we are allowed to be so but we mustn't overlook our obligation to help those that are not so fortunate. And we don't but with a global peace we can be better. There will always be unrest and tragedy as that is a part of physical life, but when the world is in democratic union, and I think that one day it must be, it will be quite a place to be, only then will we be able to fulfil Gods true destiny as freely as is possible. Which is where I think globalisation will take us. We will need to all pull together if we are to survive the future.

As these thoughts were running through him. His real thoughts were consumed by his new understandings of transience, which appeared to him as the most important aspect of human evolution. And his mind was set to bring an awareness of transient forces to the world and to validate Gods acceptance and interaction through devotion and prayer in the presence of the fourth dimension. The personal revelation that he was making, was he thought, the reason why Duncan was so eager to push him forward and back into education. It is the most important aspect of being, and that is the understanding of ones self and of ones surroundings. It was for this reason that he needed University and it was for this reason that not everyone can be a working class hero. However much they wish to be so. He had learnt that it is imperative that one finds ones place in society, and the universe, and to follow whatever proves to be the best path forward and not simply the easiest because not to do so would be to deny existing.

Chapter 4

The arena of Automatic Figural Representation that opened the door for Pete was found, like most things, by mistake. He began to see things in the 'flat areas' like the clouds or the grass, automatically laid down. The accuracy came in the figural narrative. This is what excited him the most. Narrative clearly laid down outside of his conscious but accurate to his life or life around him (current affairs). But after much practice his insight grew enough to question the intervention of an outside force of which he only knew three. Firstly his personal unconscious: secondly a collective unconscious or transient influence and thirdly Gods intervention and offering. He toyed with the idea that it was his subconscious but soon realised that it was more than that because of his belief that the subconscious does not cut in a surprising manner, it is near the conscious so it should almost be known already. With such apparently important origin he laid down as little as he could of his own conscious direction. In other words he relied on automatism right down the line in order to prove its authentic nature. However by doing this he was to rely too heavily on the accuracy of method and he soon learnt that he should begin to manipulate the images that were to have his name on. It was still the case that these paintings developed and were gradually born from automatism but that a sober mind must also be at work in case of transient error no matter how minimal.

I Won't Do Wrong

The act of not being precious with work is important as the forces that guide the figural first time around, are there for you again and always.

This knowledge began to increase his understanding and expand his mind with the questions of how, why and where, things happen and he gradually started to, not only believe in a fourth dimension, but actively live with it. The idea of living with transience made him realise that life when understood from this stand point is not a construct of mania but has purpose and Leigh lines and therefore destiny. And so he started to look back at things that he had never thought much of before and he started to see a pattern. Things seemed to have, although the construct of mania at the time, some sort of relevance and yes good decisions were made but there were bad ones too and these never accounted for much until now.

A line from a poem that he wrote many years ago;

'Do you look down from above and see manic mad moving blobs?

It suddenly seemed obvious that this was not the case. When it became clear that the air was not sterile of converse and that people are attracted to each other via transience and that mistakes can follow you around; where misrepresentation and echoes can prevent harmonic patterns. He realised that the relevance of life seemed to be easier to understand. This was however only the beginning and after much toil he decided that he should teach this manner of existence as it was a much richer one and a more worthwhile one.

Like most artists I think that understanding ones own self comes in four stages; Firstly self recognition;

Secondly community recognition; Thirdly success and realisation of ones capabilities and fourthly disillusionment or contentment of ones self understanding of personal capacity. I think Pete at this time was at stage two.

Chapter 5

He had not seen Suzie now for two years and although great friends Pete realised that it was not her fault for leaving she had vested a lot in him and though not his fault he had let her down. The truth was that she wished for more than he could offer. He had no security and yes he was at college but she knew that he would not be in a position to fulfil her requirements. They were not getting any younger and she wanted children and a house and all the things that Pete, even if he was lucky, would not be able to offer for at least five years.

Although Pete had fallen in love with his colleague Evolin she was courting and there was nothing to be done which made him sad. And although a competent student his mind set him apart from everyone else. He felt like Adam, yes he liked that name though he felt a bit sad to do so.

It was not only the power of his mind but the intricate manner in which he had suffered, but alas he was over the worst of it and with his faith in Jesus he ploughed on.

Pete now understood what his pal Duncan meant when he tried to explain the complexity of life that he had to live through in order to understand his own psyche. He had not seen Duncan and the crew for nearly two years now and he thought that the Easter before his final year show would be the perfect chance to catch up and hopefully restore his morale a little.

If things were the same then a group of his friends would be at their local drinking haunt on the Friday night, so Pete thought he would go along.

To his surprise, though he hoped she would be there, Suzie turned up along with Mat, Glen, Bob and Caroline. Pete was very happy to be there and he wished for Suzie's availability. There was no wedding ring and she did not appear to be with any of his friends but he had never seen Bob before, their body language however Pete placed in his favour.

'Hello how are Pete. How is your theory going? Do you stand any ground with the tutors yet?' Suzie asked 'I see you still have both ears.'

'Yes I have. Harder journey than I thought it was going to be. There has been a lot to learn but I think the tutors believe I am a con I don't think they believe my theory.'

'I hope you equal Freud.'

'Which one?' Pete asked for he liked both but that was Suzies point. She wished him to succeed in his own way and was leaving hope open for him. 'Lucian is Sigmund's grandson'

'Yes . . . paints birthday suits.' She added

'And the wearing of them. Yes is an amazing painter, the best. I am a student of his grandfather and am working through some of my own theories, but I do consider his analysis that every aspect of Human existence is in some way related to sexual interpretation, some what short sighted . . . 'Realising the window for a new topic. Pete looked around and asked; 'Where is Duncan? Has he moved on?'

'Yes he left for London, another baby, girl this time. They needed to be closer to their families.'

'Good for them. He was a good friend to me. And how about you are you seeing anyone?'

'Yes. Bob.'

At which point Pete felt disappointment and was momentarily washed over by an invisible transient wave, he knew that he would be but tried not to let it show.

After a couple of minutes he regained his composure.

'We are . . . expecting.'

'Well how about that, congratulations.' Pete said as he leant over to hug her, and he genuinely felt a warmth toward them both. He leaned over to Bob and simply said "congratulations" and "look after her". At that point Pete saw in Bob's eyes what he was looking for and that was all he needed. 'You're very lucky, you have a treasure here . . . two at that.'

He knew that the University course was what he had to do in order for him to be set free and realise life in order to live life to its maximum potential. This is something that everyone has to do. Some do it without any doubt of the path they are on and finding their rainbow much easier than others is their silver lining. Adversely there are those who struggle for an age to find their gold but it is there for everyone who looks hard enough and for long enough for it.

Pete sat there dazed, there was still a part of him that wished to be with Suzie, 'This should be me', he thought. He knew that he would one day sit in a similar position and so he would be happy for them, he could do nothing else. Ultimately he would have to walk the line for as long as it took. But he wanted what Bob had got, a house, a beautiful wife with baby on the way, a car and a dog from the rescue home. He would find his solace, he knew, that just not today.

Chapter 6

With only four weeks to finish college work and set up for the final year show Pete had enough work to be confident of a fairly comprehensive study of his present painterly space. With hindsight the majority were unfinished, but it was ok, they were fresh and exciting and each was like a contained moment of colour explosion interlaced with the automatic figuration that his theory and practice had uncovered. He felt that he was in as good a position as possible both academically and individually and was optimistic for his grade.

He assimilated his time there to being like a destiny walk played out in front of an audience. He had made it and he had become a different person, a better person.

He could now look forward and send out the message that all is not lost. With areas of mental health and mainly the devastating illness of schizophrenia played out before an audience, he was on a learning curve where every mistake was there to be judged and consequently compartmentalised by the psyche of the collective unconscious flux that exists in every institution. The experience was not an easy one. It was a rollercoaster, but it was completed chronologically which was his main goal. And he needed to learn the things that to be honest very few other places could have taught.

He set about explaining to whom ever it might concern everything he had learnt. He knew that his new found knowledge could help others and help is what he wanted to do. He felt that a more direct analysis could be undertaken in script, so he started to write his first book which he called 'Seventh Sense' and then changed it 'I Won't Do Wrong' because surely seventh sense is the sense of heaven.

Yes he had got a degree but it had nearly cost him his life. There was a void in his persona but he was different, full of repose and retrospect of melancholy and yet achievement. His mind seemed happier though his heart still weighed heavy. But his future was different, definitely, and he liked that.

So he choose a different path, one of peace and service to the Lord whom he now saw through a new door, the door of the fourth dimension. He would never let him go that was his duty and with his empathy for Jesus he had a friend.

'Hope springs Eternal'.

Chapter 7

Well he completed the course and could not be disappointed with a Second class degree, but he was, if only for a short while. What he had done was astronomical in retrospect and he was very happy. A tear would almost form in the corner of his eye when had he stood outside the college at the final year show, of course he shrugged this off, this was where he had often stood to smoke a cigarette in an attempt to cushion his daily worries. He cherished this moment for a short while longer before heading back to acknowledge the occasion. He knew, and liked, a lot of people there; but even after all that had happened during his time he still felt that he would have to offer a rib to find love (bare with me). A rib at this time that he could not afford to offer. He wished it to be a good rib like a strong arm not a rib that should be a burden, which at that time it just was. Would I go out with me? He asked himself, he could not say yes, though it was not his fault it was circumstance and situation. I would go out with me soon when culturally I have success and when I have caught the answer blowing in the wind, when I am seen for who I am. This he knew would take a while.

The road had been rocky and the love that he had found had been wonderful though brief. His degree had been lower than he was expecting. Even so, he was here at his graduation and he had done something, something good, and he was proud of that.

I Won't Do Wrong

After his experiences at College he was ready to embrace the life that lay ahead of him. He had been given some excellent medication for his schizophrenia and he felt for the first time that life was not necessarily conspiring against him. And although his mind was not as bright as it was, his spontaneity dampened, he vowed to strive on and forwards accepting the challenges that life and God would set before him.

In one of his paintings there was the crucifixion with an automatically narrated phenomenon, a dagger in his side this is new to religious context and Pete therefore felt empathy that the dagger was lodged in his side also. He was still in a minority a transcendental minority. He would not have children, not unless he was accepted as a writer or a painter and recognised for his intellect and culture, for if he was not then the justification of his existence would be crushed and what man can bare that.

So he set about describing how he found life, for himself and ultimately for others. When he realised the potential of educating a lost soul, as he had done his own, the chance to do his bit in the prevention of delusion in mental illness encouraged him in his fine tuning of this book with the aim to prevent mental unrest and ultimately deter crime. The education of these individuals, select few as they are, is paramount, if not for them as for the victims, by simple explanation of validity and source of delusion these victims can be saved.

In this book set out to increase awareness of mental health delusion and supernatural scepticism Pete suggests two new commandments He knows that they will make sense and due to the utmost importance of content asks himself why not if it may save a life?

Firstly the Eleventh commandment 'Don't get caught up in it.' and secondly the Twelfth Commandment 'Do Not

Take Anyone With You.' (Why would you if by doing so you are prevented from good thoughts and Heaven). These suggestions and with the title being 'I Won't Do Wrong' Pete wishes to influence people who struggle with transient knowledge and chose the name to encourage those most needy to buy the book without fear of being judged because it is diverse and everyone will like it. Transecendentiality, or being transcendental, is a science fact, an intrinsic state of mind it offers you God like powers and because of this you can be demonised. This however needn't be the case. With careful learning and good teaching this mind is easily acceptable in society. But with unfortunate circumstance or unfortunate guidance (protocol is mostly wrong) the opposite is also true. And whether it is God bestowed or something that happens sometimes. (It appears not to be a family trait though the possibility may increase I am not sure.)

Some may consider it to be—Gods greatest gift—which in itself has its hazards, in that people may think they could do a better job, or may be jealous, or may be simply annoyed that someone is taking from them interaction with God. If this is your stance then I will confirm that God will guide the transient to be one of his helpers and if the transient is upsetting anyone then God will take action. My experience does show a wave of great misunderstanding but not, any more I hope, of persecution. It is a place where self education appears, to some, as the only means of understanding a very personal world, the symptoms of which are both paranormal and supernatural.

So Pete set about creating work that would show the workings of an exposed transcendental mind, as some sort

I Won't Do Wrong

of self psycho analysis in the hope that in some way he would be able to explain his otherwise noticeable mind. The personal effects of which would prove tremendous.

Jesus has already shown total commitment in serving God as his son. The crucifixion of course should never happen again but the capacity for such loyalty in Humanity exists there. Some of which we must accept as our own.

Painting of course was important to him but every now and again he would still feel the dagger in his side; Why was . . . What if . . . Why not . . . etc. all lent themselves to a locked door. Although saying this, he himself saw the flaws in his work, his philosophies were at times a shade off. What must be understood is that with everything outside of the ego nothing is set in stone, though you can make stone of it with the egos input. Offerings the type Pete found on his canvas were just that, suggestion in other words 'transient error' should be expected. But these faults were sure to get less and less pronounced as his own studies got stronger and mindset clearer. God would surely help and that would be Pete's reward for growing as a better philosopher.

It is true that to make it in the arts one must persevere, not because you want to, but because you can not help but do anything else. And if you never receive acknowledgement from an audience then it is done for ones own salvation, and in the wider scheme of things, that is more than enough reason. And who knows some of your work may live on generations after this point and if it pleases or helps someone down the line then there are the rewards.

Pete's only motivation was the fact that he felt duty bound to educate himself in order for self acknowledgement and the acceptance of God's will. Yes it sounds a bit cliché but he needed to find himself in order to fit his transience comfortably within society and to be as beneficial to the world as his potential would allow. And that is all one must do, offer the world your all.

Chapter 8

Well all this was some time ago now and Pete had reconciled himself to never really making it as an artist, not that he would ever stop; painting or trying or something. No, more that he had more realistic ambitions, "How about this!" he said. "Sell one painting, very good, sell a few thousand books, well that is worth considering." This is some what of a silver lining where by doing the right thing for helping others he may also help himself. A man needs to earn a living and if you can do good and earn money then you can live, and that's the way it works.

Many years ago a travelling Romany gypsy sold him a table cloth and she had said to Pete that he would one day write something important. Pete had explained that she must be confusing his arts and that she meant painting, but she was adamant that she was right, he was to 'write something important'. She also saw distant shores somewhere large. Well he could see in the distant future Canada, but she thought the States 'God bless America' he could feel free there (with the right person).

At the moment he wanted a motorbike, everything else should come from continued success, small things like building with bricks one on top of the other, which seemed quite sustainable.

One day at a time. There were hard days and fine days where his only survival ethos was to pray with the birds and to try to keep walking the thin blue transient line. For a remarkably untidy man he liked order and routine, certain schedules like beer at the weekend; not too much . . ., volunteering Wednesdays and Fridays and regular jobs gardening and helping. His wild cards were painting and motor mechanics. He did these whenever the urge took him. One thing that he did notice was those five minute jobs that never seemed to get done, when left on the back burner for too long led him to depression, so easily corrected and he found that the occasional royal kick up the backside was sometimes worth applying. He had learned these traits of his mind and kept reminding himself of them.

The next few years were hard there were good times but also bad, highs and lows and he wondered whether he was becoming more depressed as his understanding of the restrictions that schizophrenia imposed became clearer. He still had his dream which his mind often referred too. He still enjoyed sitting in a light rain and watching bats fly close to him at dusk. But the closer he got to his dream the further away it seemed to be. He still believed that he would find his rainbow. He just hoped that the gold would not have been stolen. He had his right rib still to give so he enjoyed life to the full trying his best to follow the critique that he had laid down in his book 'I Won't Do Wrong' which he still hoped would be a true survival manual for transcendental thought. A book that he hoped would act as a buoyancy aid, like a life jacket, which he thought would be just enough to see anyone through the worst times.

He had a small house 'out in the sticks' and he had loved doing it up and renovating it as much by himself as with others. He had his classic car and his motorbike and a small studio in the garden for his art work, which although not selling like hot cakes were selling and he had shown them at some good galleries and acquired a certain respect

I Won't Do Wrong

for what he does. His next goal was to exhibit in London. He had a sizable amount of work and he really needed to be recognised by the London art scene. He felt worthy of his talent and its recognition, not only for himself but also for his girlfriend, whom he wished to please.

(O.K. this bit is in the future but hopefully not too far into it!).

It was early days but he would love to go off on the motorbikes and travel to France. He was yet to get his licence and indeed finish building the classic bike that he had purchased very reasonably as a job lot of parts. As an able mechanic but an amateur one he would spend endless hours on its construction whilst he hoped that acquiring a licence would not prove more than a small stumbling block. His road awareness was good and he was a sensible car driver. One thing he knew was that he was into the bike as a path of nostalgia and not a toy for adrenalin though the two would inevitably cross not too frequently he hoped. His dream was good and he wished to live it.

All the way through the last summer, through winter and spring the SAD (seasonal affective disorder) had not shown itself to him. He was confused as to whether he suffered from it or not. He had decided not, but with the coming of the summer months his mood had lifted, basking was good and the long warm days seemed to offer him more than he was expecting.

(Back to the present)

Volunteering as a gardener and a decorator kept him in touch with his faith in Humanity and usually yes it really was/is a joy.

Life as you know throws challenge upon challenge, which he knew how to manage and indeed was the source of enlightenment. The accompanying mental agility was like a breath of fresh air; keeping his step light. Happy memories is what he was after and his heart remained buoyant as he awaited recognition. For his truth lay where the sun shone on an afternoon. Of course unity was a goal, but to sit amongst the birds and the bees was enough . . . enough of a challenge at least! Its basis being one of continual dialogue expressing compassion and acceptance from God's nature, which is always there to be heard, talked too or listened too.

"Life's not so bad in fact I think that it is rather marvellous." He said under his breath.

To be mortal that was his ultimate goal. Of course he was mortal but there was an essence about him, that of transcendentiality that weighed four times on his shoulders. How nice life would be 'to be normal' he thought, still he hung onto the ethos that he might have volunteered for his intrinsic state, and this alone created a premise that he would have to explain why he did not try to use this state for the good of the world. And so he would do his best.

His art was going well and he still saw himself in the garden of his house in the country, the one that he had not yet managed to acquire, but it was there if only in his dreams. This he could see whilst basking in the sun. You can be anywhere laying quietly on the grass in the heat of the sun.

He had bought a motorbike built in the year of his birth, it was in a thousand pieces but he yearned for the day that it worked and the excursions he envisaged.

His dreams seemed to be closer than ever before and he wondered whether he should try to promote his book on a television chat show or not (given half a chance). He had a very nice doctor who had offered to read it and offer some sort of analysis, hopefully in the form of blurb for the back cover. This was of paramount importance to have the book checked for authenticity whether positive or negative. It needed an anchor of some sort.

He hoped that he had done enough to promote this book as a 'manual' for the understanding of some aspects of schizophrenia for those who suffer and are keen to learn and to offer insight to family members and doctors.

It would seem a shame if the knowledge of this book, that had been at the core of his recovery, should be left alone and not offered to those who had enough about them to read and understand it. Pete had done it and he thought others could as well. Of course this idea is heavily biased, it was after all one persons calculations and observations so if it was not bias then it would hardly have been worthwhile writing.

Pete was determined to remove the metaphorical dagger from his side and even clean and sew the wound himself, if only to prove that he could do it and that he wanted to.

Having said that the support, especially in the latter years, from the medical staff, staff that he admired greatly, had helped a huge amount and were true diamonds of the profession.

Chapter 9

All things considered Pete had found himself in a contented position. It is the most bizarre thing he thought and as he tried to express his situation he began to realise the importance of moving. If you can imagine for one moment that there were microphones set up all around you and they not only hear you but are actually judging through an invisible speaker. And that these judgements are continual and for everyone to hear and there is no room for tumble weed. Well it is quite a scary place to be but it is also negotiable if not hard work, one must learn to conduct a symphony with all transient knowledge. The main constant in the countryside is the bird population broadcasting every thought and sometimes answering them. He often wondered if St. Francis of Assisi was so burdened for he was known as the Saint that talked with birds. This is where his daily challenges started; where sensory over load can be a constant obstacle.

The majority is complementary and about faith of God and natures faith in me, for there are plenty of compliments. Essential God rewards good thought and the birds are there to remind us. If this sits heavy with you try to remember that 'Hope Springs Eternal' and you can't turn that off (so long as you are true to yourself and God).

Pete as it happens represents a life much like my own and I have used his name to allow me to get closer to the story of these few important years of my life.

I Won't Do Wrong

Do many things that is the answer. I am fortunate I have the opportunity to paint and write and work on my bike and car, many are not so fortunate. I do pronounce myself as one of the most transcendental men in all the world (intrinsically that is), and it is for these reasons I have been able to calculate and hopefully add to a pool of knowledge of literature that may help some by making their personal research easier so that their time spent self educating may be fruitful. My opportunity to do many great things has not yet past. I will do my best and so can you. I must therefore do what I can in the name of research and peace to the best of my ability. And my ability is best expressed through theology and psychology, formatting theories which can be easily read and understood.

Chapter 10

Strange as it seems my understanding of the differences in religions remained naïve and yet religion is at the core of most souls, so I started to research and found out enough to form a basic understanding. So to those who are not sure as I was, I will explain what I found out.

Transubstantiation is one that divides the two main Christian religions who's core difference is that The Catholic Church demand that transubstantiation is a truth, and this is not only a doctrine of the communion bread and wine but to every instance of its form. Conversely the Anglican Church sees such things as representations of a fact and not therefore a fact in themselves. Now my understanding and explanation can be expressed with the analogy of voice hearing, where transubstantiation can be at its most organic. OK but as I have explained in previous chapters there are cases of folly and cases of mentelepathy. It is therefore no wonder that there is a divide in opinion. Both perspectives are correct but both can also be wrong. So in my view 'which one is correct?', they both are.

Now I can not leave this without expressing my theory of the coming of Jesus and his immaculate conception. I am convinced that there is literature in the Vatican that is inaccessible to most and because of this and simply through my own intellectual curiosity I have stumbled on a theory that I wish to express. Because I think a lot of people may shy away from the church through a lack of knowledge and

I Won't Do Wrong

belief in this one event, which they should not need to do, I aim to ease their path toward God through a theory of my own expressing both the importance and unimportance of this one stumbling block or marvel. I for one do not mind if Jesus was born through immaculate conception or not. What I do mind is people being put off by this apparent paradox because I know that it is Jesus and our Lord that have saved so many including myself.

So this is where I started I wish not to cause doubt in the Catholic faith and their belief in an immaculate conception it is the same as the Anglican belief. It is myself that is lacking in belief but I do not think that should matter in terms of my support and belief in the Christian faith.

But this is where I was thinking; If in the Catholic faith one must accept that the bread and the wine actually turn into the body and blood of Christ then we must also perhaps accept that Jesus may be the son of God in the same way. In other words that there was no immaculate conception and that he is the son of God by the devotion of Gods choosing. This opposes protestant thought that somehow God created Jesus with no help from man. To go a little further and to explain a difference within the Christian church one must consider the difference in prayer. Catholic prayer is directed through the most appropriate saint and not simply through God and his son Jesus. This again is distancing themselves from the one whom only God was the father.

Will there be a second coming? If so who are waiting or expecting? The easiest place to start is with Judaism who's people believe there will be a Messiah but that it was not Jesus. So they are awaiting for a God filled man in order for them to have their national borders written as from God. They already have national boundaries set out by the allies after WW2 but this design was not from God.

Christians believe there will be a second coming

Islam is different in this aspect as they believe Jesus to be a prophet much like Mohamed was so they are expecting more prophets but they will prefer to follow Mohamed as he is their favourite one. Once this door is opened we must start thinking what else can any one person do? Will he be called a modern world prophet and be praised for his intrinsic make up and devotion to God or will his greatness only be experienced when the day of judgement is upon us. Will he be there to help us in our most desperate of times in order to guide us toward heaven. I hope so.

I for one know the importance of the first coming for me it is Jesus and God that has had served me in my recovery and my very essence of living. Now to live without him would be punishing and not a place I would like to be. The same I am sure relates to Mohamed' followers where the very knowledge of his existence is enough to put one foot in front of the other. No the important distinction that must be made is that of realising the parallel relevance of each faith and treating each person who has a respective faith the same loyalty as those in the same faith. That is of course if they consider Human kind and God merciful and good.

Of course we will wonder why the world is not at peace if the Messiah has already been here to explain ultimate enlightenment. My view must say that there may be critics but what he did no man will ever do again, 'Was he the son of God?' Yes he was, though his DNA would not have said so. His transience allowed him to be the son of God. It is certainly the way he lived. He was the holder of the holy grail, and that alone with the conviction of sincerity, led him to die as God's only son. And that is to be admired and remembered, and utilised for his strength and undying

I Won't Do Wrong

servitude is there for salvation. And my view. There will never be anyone like Jesus but there may be someone who can answer the question of everything which I hope is just as good. But emotionally and morally in my book Jesus rules. It is Jesus who saved me and many others and if you can open your door to him he will save you as well.

I also feel in a position to prove that some of the miracles of Jesus were exactly that. He must have been ten times more transcendental than me. And I, as every transcendental, have the ability to affect transience in a profound manner. So it is the pure possibility of transcendental healing that Jesus proved, and he did so in the form of prayer. Now I'm not sure whether Mohamed did miracles, though I suspect he did, and he also did his work in the sight of prayer realising the importance of thought, so like them we must also pray for cognitivety as well as for our sins and our wishes.

The Muslim faith does not encourage narrative empathy, this religion is a place where the art created for its worship has no narrative nor figuration. Instead complex patterns in mosaic or factorial form, encourages a trend of trance that allows the body to feel an accountable euphoric state, touching the Holy Spirit. In effect the art is a tool for prayer, as in Christianity, the difference is that the Muslim communication is with something that no man could ever understand but which is to be marvelled and praised. Where the Christian art communicates through the suffering of his son Jesus and the saints that followed, which allows us a tangible link with Human empathy. And by association allows prayer to be more direct to Human existence as its prayer is channelled through his son who of course was Human.

So this barrier that divides us from God has here been bridged as his son was Human and God therefore knows how suffering feels, which leads us less required to show our belief as he knows how we feel. There is a paramount of importance to pray as we know prayer is actualising and does work (Re ch placebo effect). So to those who pray the five times a day I commend and admire and I love the idea that the animals deserve dignity in death I think they do too.

I can not pass without expressing how important it is to know that Jesus represents everyone of us who offers themselves to be seen. And the ultimate promise is that we would do our best in the face of suffering and keep faith with determination, that is an unspoken Christian vow.

For a bit of background knowledge; Jesus is recognised in the Muslim faith as a prophet much like Mohamed, but Mohamed lived about six hundred years after Jesus and showed to the Muslim people a preferred prophet. The fact that the Muslim faith follow Mohamad's word, as well as but more than, the word of Jesus to me is simply a parallel philosophy. They both offer a perfection for the praise of God's word and a way through life that is the most honourable to God and to man with the hope of acceptance after death. But that Christianity offers more insight into human suffering on earth offering salvation whilst alive rather than gifts of bounty after death. No we are here in the physical world where material things are the building blocks of life. The next world I believe will be very different somewhere that we can be granted absolution and harmony and perfection so long as we live on earth as caring selfless people. The difference between the Christian and Muslim faiths lies simply in the form of communication and method. Christianity I believe offers the congregation an empathy for Jesus's position and God an empathy for Human suffering through his son. And that ultimately the

Muslim faith offers divine enlightenment for a congregation of servers through high philosophy and intellect. Now I know some of the pressures of being transcendental and the responsibility is sometimes hard to bear. I also know the importance of thought.

(This bit is superstition)

An interesting reflection of perspective on the outlook of life as we know it lies in an equally balanced reversal of objectivity. This point has been made on simple analysis where the Islam and Hebrew write backward from right to left and from back to forward things like the capital of Iraq is named Baghdad and not Goobdad where the oppressors in Iraq are called Sunnies and the allied sector called the Sheits, and where the Hamas are much less favourable than the Fatas.

I have written the last paragraph to show that there is always a potential for parallel ideological arena's whether they be a positive and a negative (Like in photography) where we can see from both perspectives of reality. What I have said here is less than correct but the idea that I was chasing was that there lie within our world branches of theology that get support from Allah or God. What this entails is that there is room for bubbles of belief and support with the raw materials that are given to us by the Lord. Seeds that grow from good, producing more good in an escalatory notion until you have two things that are equally as good nurtured on the same stuff but very different. Similar to evolution through separation (Darwin).

I believe that with this understanding we may learn to live knowing that this is possible.

Chapter 11

It feels strange to me to say this but I truly believe that I have started a new chapter in my life. I can assimilate it as though life is a corridor and there have always been many doors but up till now they had either been locked or strangely sealed, some of which now swing open not with emergency but just allowing me to peep in and explore if the wish so falls on me to do so.

One of these doors will be my optimum route and I am hoping that it will involve my art and my writing. It seems similar to 'Of Mice and Men' by J Steinbeck. I hope and plead though that my aim for a house on the hill does not turn out the same as the tepidly unfortunate destinies walk as those who were there then walked.

Television may play a role as it always has done with or without my knowledge. To be the other side of the camera. I wonder who I will see? May be someone I know? I feel that it would be the right thing to do, to answer the ever foreboding quest to promote myself and ideas that are prominent in my ever so vague political mind, a basic sense of wrong and right. To steer the finest vessel I can build to all the lands and to all the places especially those that might have been overlooked. It will be a vessel of explanation and of justice and of knowledge much like the missionaries have already done and do. For the fourth dimension to be understood is my ultimate goal. And ultimately to be an ambassador of fair play.

Shooting Star

It was his first taste of freedom and he had grabbed it with both hands. His life was going to start today. He was convinced of that. All of his misgivings must end and he must be dead straight. His nerves though were in tatters, but were somehow sewn together in a random but tight net of which there were few holes. The sparks that he generated were of the strongest in nature and were soon recognised by most that knew him.

Smoking of the deadly weed was a day to day habit. It increased his mood to be free and to have a free spirit, which increased his esteem for there had always been too many rules in his life. Because of this boost he was more spontaneous and more likable. This new machine was pretty nifty though he knew very little about it. His cognitive life was played on a fine frequency, though he would never acknowledge that fact as it lay too close to the void that he had created in order to accept sanity.

People were his prime concern but his greatest wonder was the whole of the earth and the enormity of space. Concern should have been a little closer to home though. But hey it was the early nineties and these things could be learned later. The most important thing was integration and acceptance. This he was good at acquiring for he was genuinely caring and concerned. The only thing that betrayed him was his inability to draw lines. And when he did draw them he fully and observably trod right over them, for his judgment seemed to change with his mood. And what I mean by this is complex but simple. He judged everything with little hindsight. It was a case of 'actual situation' all the time with no reference to 'situation actually' (Re Ch) and boy what a fool he made of himself. His philosophy was 'higher is better' and he did get high. This gave him paranoia and the things that he once took for granted he found he no longer understood. His mind was now questioning the surgery he had whilst young for correction of behaviour.

Let the surgery wait is all I can offer and I will talk about this for a while. For a troubled soul there is always a starting place. A place where actually he has been born again. Young enough not to remember any thing else, and the maintenance of this, memory-denied-automaton is correction, by surgery and the installation of more evidence of an unjust situation. This catastrophic impairment of the brain caused lack of memory and apparently reasonable justification of his actions and consequently the aggressive instinct surfaced as the fight in him grew. This can however be countered by a regular assessment, by which I mean simply saying 'do you know why . . . 'If this is not done early and continued you will have trouble. If this is not countered with cognitive treatment it could lead to trouble. I call it 'being locked out'. Take heed these words they are from my own mind there are no winners which is why I have taken it upon myself to say 'let the surgery wait'. All things considered I am very transcendental by nature and am therefore somewhat of an anomaly but if you treat my case as an experiment then the results are in my living and a reason for hope.

It is for these reasons and an apt ability to find fun that he lost focus and became somewhat of a drifter at senior school and further education, always wanting to chase the rainbow and getting pretty close to it at times. Accountably the sun went in before he found the pot of gold, and so it should have done for a man without God is no man at all.

Anyway the story went a bit like this:

Chapter two

In room number thirteen the quest for a different future lay ahead of him. It started with a joint (which he enjoyed a lot already) so he immediately felt strong positives and an empathy for future days. These were the soundest people that he could have wished to have been with, and if he was to succeed then this is where it would start.

The first few weeks were terrific fun and there was always some one to smoke with, many different personalities congregating just to chill out. At this stage he still had a budget to stick too and he did stick to it. The first payment for halls was paid and he could afford to live well with food every day supplied at the canteen all inclusive, he was not going to starve.

To be honest he was quite a good student in the first term. He had many allies who were excellent friends. If only he had partaken in the course after February. He had decided to take the day off for his birthday, but got stuck in a grove and it was at that point where he knew he was opting out so he never really went back. His life was consumed by freedom that he had never known before. It was round about this time when he took his first ecstasy tablet. Well he had had a half of one before but this was an altogether different experience.

The euphoria was immense he was so high 'too high', after all what is left if you have already experienced euphoria to an extent that will never be equalled. Well I will tell

I Won't Do Wrong

you; stability, love and God (which come together) and philosophy.

Dancing and dancing where it is not a boy and girl thing but a common collective conscious. E for euphoria and speed for the energy he had got it all pretty worked out. His life however was slipping away from under his feet. With his feelings of inadequacy hidden, like a foreign bank account gaining interest, he started to show signs of instability like a balloon that every one could see except himself. His memory was in a place in his mind that he did not have the key for.

Yes well he failed his course at the end of year exams, but accepted the challenge laid down to all those who had failed to ensure entrance into the re-sit's. Which was to draw a technical plan of a foot bridge using the knowledge that had been acquired over the year. So off he went to the town library to get some plans of a foot bridge. The only one he found covered many pages and was in imperial measurements. Simple conversions were required, but it took him a long time and was damn near perfect, but a futile exercise, as I'm sure that he knew because his subject knowledge was poor as his lack of attendance and poor studentship should have already told him. His study there had finished.

Chapter three

He did however have some very wonderful times one of which included a time after the nightclub we went to a ruined church where he and two friends climbed the walls and sat to watch the sun rise and the stillness of the night, simply smoking and being tranquil. They were up on the walls when some rather drunk students came into the grounds. There was some banter, good stuff, and they decided to come and join us.

Now I might have looked cool up there but he was terrified that our inebriated compatriots would fall, and that idea wasn't worth thinking. I simply prayed with every thing I had to keep them from falling (as one of them nearly did). But they didn't and thank God that was the way it went. That aside it was one of the most interesting and beautiful experiences that he wished to repeat but never did.

He did experiment with hallucination and it was here at the church that he saw a carriage being towed across the sky in all its brilliance headed by must be twelve horses, of course he wished to share this experience but being so personal a vision this could not be shared. There was one more notable hallucination which occurred in a chill out room at one of my favourite clubs, it was a vision similar to that of the Sistine Chapel, where a wise man with beard (synonymous with God) was stretching out his hand toward a cherub their fingers nearly touching. Of course we are all God's children so I felt quite empowered by this,

I Won't Do Wrong

fortunately snapping out of it just in time for the bouncer who was watching decided he had had enough.

He used to leave the clubs steaming, quite literally, to the amusement of those around him. It was sure as ever a good work out.

He had bad times as well and remembered going to a drinking club and was acting the fool. He was in love but because of his paranoia, and the deceitful nature of his freak he lost his mind. Truth being that the explanation of his situation had been lost due to his large narcotic consumption and his huge transience which made him feel as normal as everyone else, although he wasn't. He was good in bed though his first time rendered some improvement. In reason the fact that it wasn't perfect bothered him immensely as he was in love. As John Lennon said 'its all dick'. This was unknown territory for him and he wished that he had had a level playing field to draw from. His quest for a healthy life was about to start.

This is the part where I tell you all the unjust of the protocol that had been enforced upon him and the lack of the for's and the why's and where's that encompassed his freak. All he knew was that he was not the same as anyone else though through nurture or nature he was not sure. In fact it was both, one ultimately disguising and confusing the other.

Now that he had lost everything he had to ask why. So he became interested in human psychology. And I wish that it could have ended there but it didn't. He was rubbish at psychology and didn't even grasp the idea that he was transcendentally more powerful than anyone else. My ideologies said that everyone is made the same, and of course in the eyes of God we are, but in the eyes of physics we all have our individuality. It would however be years before he could call himself a responsible voice hearer. Having been diagnosed with schizophrenia he set himself the task of working out this illness so that he could lead as normal a life as possible, but it was hard work and he nearly didn't make it a few times. But I have now and that is down to the care that I have received and the people that I have met, but also through self education and the literature that I have read. This goes hand in hand with having the right mind to understand which at last he had. Along side this I have been experimenting with voice hearing, flaws and truths, until I satisfied myself with what I now call reality. (Re; ch 'Voice hearing').

Before he went for hospital treatment, he got a job in a store in town where he did everything he could to be competent but he was lost like a fish out of water. His senses were all peaking and he was looking for hidden cameras and stuff. And it would take a long time before he could sort out his transient world so that he could simply live with his senses. He was diagnosed with schizophrenia though he knew perfectly well that there was more to this than just delusion. He had not worked it out but to his satisfaction he would do. And now he has done but only sufficiently so on his discovery of a new revelation which is that along side the body there is a complimentary spirit, which is just as capable of converse out of the physical mind as in (where in is called mentelepathy) I am happy (Re Ch 'Voice Hearing'). The difference in my experience of hearing voices comes, as everything else I believe in, to be scientific. So the existence of a spirit that is partially separated from the physical allowing for Mentelepathy (a state of trans telepathy that is real to both respondants), and folly (a state of trans telepathy real to only the listener due to the spirit of the voice sender being in the 'Ultra World').

I Won't Do Wrong

The combination of these states of transtelepathy gives me both empathy and solace. My conclusion was, well, conclusive. This but of course is confusing and I feel that it is down to me to say why. The reason for the confusion is that the spirit voice doesn't know if it is acting without the transients knowledge, so the state of mentalepathy is undistinguishable 99% of the time, which opens the doors to folly. If we combine this with the fact that transcendental minds have the ability to affect voices as he does non speak, we end up with a thick purple soup that can be very toxic. You can drown in it or be poisoned by it, which is why I am here explaining it. It is quite lethal and needs explaining to prevent the psychosis that is fed on it.

Chapter four

The reason for this book is to shed light on schizoid behaviour in an attempt to reduce its occurrence simply through basic understanding and awareness of abstract traits. To offer hope to those most helpless. In essence I am only adding to the already vast knowledge that only literature can hold. And that is it really. I explained it this way in this book to throw those floating in the purple soup a life line, an offering like a life jacket to keep the sufferer buoyant until times get better which with faith they will do, because education is where it's at.

I think that what I am saying is 'give someone enough fuel and at some point they will want to expel it all at once.' so cut down on the fuel.

So I was a bit crazy, I know that now. Either I had no fear or bucket loads of it. It didn't make sense although I was quite a capable person. Certainly I could put things in a rational way and I tried too because I knew that everyone there were guiding their ships through the changing seas of university in order to be enriched and to progress with their lives. The confusion lay with my uncapped transcendental mind, a mind sadly without God or more reasonably without an understanding of the ways of God. And that is why I am writing. I hope that I have given reason for some of my more crazy antics and that although my grave had been dug I have tunnelled out and feel born again by doing so.

I Won't Do Wrong

It was not all so rosy toward the end of this particular era. Mental health is all so hard to deal with and it is not only tough on the patients but also on those around them.

I will end with a poem that I wrote to express my disappointment and a willingness to explain my simple philosophy. In essence the time is right to draw a line and say I was there but now I am here. Thank you;

> Look up from below
> There is a shooting star.
> Whizzing across the sky,
> A spectacle, a marvel.
> But how it has landed
> It's a rock,
> Which viewed . . .
> From the side
> Has left a scar . . .
> And a hollow.
> Echo.

Four Dimensions

After watching Steven Hawking talking on the Universe and in particular other dimensions of it I have come to a decision that the transience and inter relationship of a sixth sense is in fact the evidence of a fourth dimension.

Having experience of leaving my body (subject to my belief) as I was somewhat inebriated, and living with high transience, it has become a very relevant question as to whether we are on the verge of discovering a fourth dimension, which could be taught alongside the conventional teaching of the three we know of in the physical world.

Not only would this be the answer to a lot of the questions surrounding schizophrenia, but the Ultra World when understood could be I am sure the knowledge that could stop all vengeance.

Everything must be powered or generated from somewhere (at the start of the universe) so why not from a fourth dimension?. The clues are in our physical universe. Black holes I feel are an example of energy transfer, where space is concentrated so much so that when mass is infinitesimally small and equally infinitely heavy (known as a singularity) there may occur a 'quantum leap' creating new galaxies else where in the universe or this could be the source of energy for the fourth dimension.

This leads me to one of the physicists greatest conundrums, the question of gravity, which is; 'Why does

I Won't Do Wrong

it appear so weak compared to the other forces? Forces that it shared equilibrium with before the big bang. Those being thermal radiation, nuclear radiation, the internal forces of the atom, and magnetism.

My theory is that everything in the universe has gravity (even light feels gravity). So before the big bang, where all of natures forces were equal and balanced, it took the gravity of everything to be so. But the other forces do not need in the same way other matter to be whole. In other words gravity looses power via separation. The smaller quantity of something required for the maximum force means that each quantum of that force is stronger and so in relation has less lost in separation. So in proportion these other forces (which are not in everything but only in themselves and their like) like nuclear radiation and magnetism have a smaller material equity in comparison and therefore the percentage mass per force is so outweighed that there appears a stark contrast in their relative strengths. This along with the knowledge that gravitational force is localised, so the further the finite pool of gravitational matter (everything in the universe) disperses the weaker is its accumulative effect though the more stable the localised range. As the further the matter disperses the weaker the effect until eventually there will be only an infinitesimally small effect on its distant cousin. I think we can reasonably suggest where the apparent loss of energy has gone. It has diminished because it relies on everything to be whole. Other energies like the energy of the very small have a smaller equity of matter ie they rely on themselves and their like and so because of this equity balance gravity seems to lose more strength. The internal forces of the atom is the best example of how gravity is lost in separation because it is the opposite, it doesn't. It relies not on other matter simply and only on the atoms that it bonds. They may be affected by thing such as heat or chemical reaction but their stable force remains constant through time.

However I quite like the idea expressed by Steven Hawking when he suggested that the lack of gravitational force is due to the requirements of a fourth dimension. Which is a definite possibility after all what is a singularity? (For those not sure where a singularity occurs it is at the centre of a black hole and is so small as to be infinitesimal and yet so heavy that it sucks in even light.) It could be some sort of portal or an energy source for the fourth dimension. I think it is more likely to be a portal transferring energy around the universe. Just maybe. Now scientists talk of the very big and the very small so if we take quantum physics where something can appear at two places at nearly the same time perhaps all of this gravity, so strong that it sucks even light in, reappears somewhere else in the universe as something else? This is only theory but it is good to ask questions.

The next obvious question must be; 'What is in this fourth dimension?' It is possible to suggest that along with extra dimensions of our physical world there may also be parallel universes. A place noticeably cut off from our existence in our universe. Of course Heaven with a place for the spirit to go, a place where we may pass onto, a place that will be enlightening may be one but there may be more or even many more. The reason I feel strongly of this place is that I have left my body before and existed only as a spirit proving to me that our bodies are vessels for a spirit. I am sure that it was not simply hallucination so sure in fact that

I Won't Do Wrong

I am compelled to encourage this belief in a parallel universe and the possible life without the physical.

I am here to explain our fourth dimension. Some people will be aware of the Sixth Sense and Jung has suggested the existence of a 'collective unconscious'. I call this arena the Ultra World. A place almost indistinguishable from conscious thought. A place where the spirit may go to unconsciously and act individually from conscious thought without the knowledge of doing so. And it shows itself 'this other place' by its related folly.(re ch Voice hearing)

I have been interested in the idea of infinity and as to whether it has an ending point. The theory is that if it is never ending any possibility would have its stage. So for example; probability states that though unimaginable there is a probability that there is life exactly the same as ours on Earth with people acting exactly the same and living in exactly the same way experiencing everything that we do. Now the idea that infinity is never ending would state that this is not only possible but probable.

I on the other hand believe that the infinity of something has its ending, a place where there is nothing left to represent. This theory is backed up by the scientific belief that different infinities are different sizes. Which if true is clear proof of my theory.

Does God exist?

Theories such as 'transient timing' and 'transient response', things of the superstitious, supernatural and things Biblical say yes. I like to put science to Biblical events and I find the possibility of transient timing is the most exciting thing:

'The Hebrews and the timing that the Red Sea which was drawn back to let the Israelites across. Modern theory suggests that the crossing was further north and that there was evidence of a tsunami at about that time. This to me proves the existence of transient timing. Where God could not have stopped the tsunami but that he knew to tell the Israelites to get a move on. This is perfect and proves the existence of God, his relationship with the world and his relationship with us.'

Now the physicists believe enough to suggest the existence of up to eleven different dimensions. This number appears to be out of the blue but I think what they mean is that there is capacity for there to be a lot. And I know that there could be but I can only find evidence of one 'The Ultra World' But I have belief in the parallel universe of Heaven and possibly a different one for Hell, so there may be eleven? But not dimensions, universes. I suggest that dimensions that do not directly affect life in our universe are not relative dimensions but parallel universes in other words they are not food for fodder but pose for intellect. We can only deal with tangibility. God of course is in Heaven and he talks to us possibly through the Ultra World using the fourth dimension. This seems the most likely link. He is tangible. He is real. He is gracious. I am a great believer in science and so am very aware of the intricacies of the holy spirit. My belief is that there is only one God but that the holy spirit is the conductor of a multitude of personal holy experiences, so I also know that God is personal. And the link for me is our collective unconscious. Some say that God has mirrored our spirits from his own. And I know that God would be with me anywhere in our universe and so he must have an intrinsic medium of contact where he can converse with an individual. So I think it is likely to be through our fourth dimension the Ultra World which we are all connected to wherever we are. It might be comparable to a radio link but must be in my view more personal and slightly less tangible but without problems of the physical

(i.e. it won't break or loose reception). So it is possible in that way that Heaven is in contact with Earth. It may be the stuff that connects all of Gods Worlds. It may be dark matter (the latest scientific conundrum). We know that it is there but cannot perceive its form. We shall have to wait and see.

God's Word

I think that the latest phenomenon must be the continuity of God's Word, in our ever changing world. All of our religions have script descended from God him self and their validity is not questioned because we all see how it is possible to hear God on a personal level. However we are all not sure how it is that we can turn this sensation into the actual words of God. It takes a prophet to do this. That we can accept. And so the question must be; will Gods word change tone and offer different truths with the passing of time and life? To answer this we need examples to analyse and to try and reach a conclusion. To me the obvious example should be the killing of our animals for food. We know that in Islam the animal must be killed the same described way called halal and we also know that Judaism like their meat killed in the right way cushdie. This practice, at the time of Mohamed, was crucial in the balance that we live with nature. It was a discipline that rendered the Muslim folk compassionate. There are places still today that could do with this Muslim trait. But in the west we have scientifically the best way to kill and the least suffering way and so now that technology, has changed and there are more options on the table than when God made his declaration surely his guidance may change over time in a reflection of changed circumstances? God knows some voodoo preachers should use such guidance, but do we all nowadays with our faith in the modern abattoir, which however repulsive is more

Humane than to slaughter in a more traditional manner. So as long as we are doing our best, because the death of an animal should always be prayed for and we do this by killing as quickly and cleanly as possible, so that the animal spirit may continue on to heaven's side of existence and hopefully chew the cud on Gods favourite pastures.

So with the confusion of the Holy spirit with its wide reaching arms, arms that can find you wherever you hide, arms that can cure you with their words and arms that can make you feel like you're the only person he has time to talk to, are set here for us to philosophise over. It seems that only a few can go past the holy spirit and actually talk to God and when they do they leave a legacy, but we must always be ready to acknowledge the truth; which is that God's Word may change depending on circumstance and what sort of water has passed under the bridge and to what sort of situation a modern man finds himself. And so to not accept change even a change of the way we see God himself we must be neighbouring on walking blind. So long as we know that God is gracious and that we may be compassionate and kind we can work the rest out.

Book 2

Observations

Dual Dialogue And The Super Ego

Sigmund Freud categorised the mind into three levels of consciousness; the Id, the Ego and the Superego. Where the Id is a subconscious level of thought; the Ego is the part of the personality structure that deals with external reality and controls the power of the Id, whilst the Superego is one that records punishment, so that one comes to operate instinctively from past events.

I have come to a decision that the Superego as a Freudian theory suggests an audible response with the spoken word, possibly a response from the Id, but also a possible interjection from the ego. The character of the superego acts with suggestion, correction or notification of what resides in the Id or what wants to be interjected from the ego (normally this response is from the Id and it is from the Id that Freud works). In other words there is a response which is audible and yet not the physically spoken or chosen word.

This is often an involuntary response and its content is reliant on a number of underlying stresses which reside in the Id, so it is therefore affected by ones state of mind. With this knowledge one may begin to direct ones sobriety toward being the person that he or she wishes to be. (With the new wisdom of this new arena one may need to work for a while to balance ones Zen. This is expected).

Such realisation of a new channel of converse can lead to paranoia. Suddenly you are aware of the existence of this other converse which is seemingly out of the ego's immediate control. You will wonder what it is saying and therefore worry. Cope as best as you can is a very good way to start, and try to align the Superego's response with the Ego's required direction. One must be patient, but all this is possible and will become second nature with time. And when you have enough experience you will begin to be able to predict superego response and be at one with your Zen allowing it to become a valid part of your personality.

In its purest form it can be like talking in tongues where the conversation is based only sincerely on the super ego's content. This happens only very rarely and is quite an eyrie experience.

The transcendental mind can morph all manner of non speak. And the superego is merely another platform of converse and is therefore malleable to the transient. It is however a more spontaneous converse and offers itself up for change less easily especially with regard to his own superego and there will need to be a particular pause of reflection for realisation of any change. Normally he will not strain to this extent but the theory is real and available for use as in most other converse. What I mean by this is that he may have the strength to change something that is said, if he is convinced that an amendment need take place (re ch.; Ninety-Nine Percent). This is an asset. Oppositely though the transient may morph things that are fine into something unwanted simply by mishearing or worrying or just getting it wrong. This is on the worst side of being transient (re. ch. Transient Error). He will wonder what was said and what

I Won't Do Wrong

would correct his misinterpretation and in the process get himself in a tangle and there lays his transient trap.

So this theory is valid for all the audible world but the superego is an area that is least likely to be changed by the transient. Because of this intrinsic purity the Superego remains at the acute end of transient error. In that it is most damaging to the transient because it is regarded as the most honest of converse. He will therefore feel out of cognitive control, which can be soul destroying. But with the ability to train yourself it also offers, when cognitive, a good cushion in converse as it helps to oil the cogs of the ego with relevant and appropriate assistance. This I argue is its reason for being.

For someone who has been locked out, by which I mean someone who has travelled the journey of their life but who have no concept of transient patterns, the introduction of the superego will be unsettling. But as I have said you can learn its character, as I have done. It may take some time but it is a worthwhile transition as it opens the doors to other possibilities including the subtleties of God's world which understandably you may not have sensed before.

I will put forward here that the Superego may transgress an individuals knowledge. By which I mean it may say something relevant, something that he/she could not have known. Such as; 'shame about that close call (in the car)' on welcoming someone to their house. (Where there actually was a close call.) but how could he have known?

Reading Between The Lines; Concentration and association

Some times it is possible that one may read a text and instead of absorbing the content and following the narrative, every word can seem like some sort of transient response. In effect the book can act as a medium between the 'Ultra World' and the Physical World creating a dialogue that is not written in words. When this is done the text and the 'dialogue' have only the medium (the book) in common. This I feel is a symptom of 'transient transgression' by which I mean that you are instinctively searching for the correct transient path, but that you are seeing too many transient patterns. This can be a sign that you are peaking in a transcendental state so much so that you have been distracted from reality. This can be a sign that all is not as well as it should be. Like most theories that I work with I write this with first hand experience. Of course I followed this line of transience all the way to the fence and it is very trying and destructive. One must realise that time is offered to us and if you want to read then you should and transience will allow you to, even if it is in small chunks at a time. You will finish the book, in your own time and you are not being tested on it so you get what you can from it, which may only show in the success of completion but that is good. There is lots to read and you will find that, as with everything that I promote, success will be fruitful and a key for you to get back on track, small steps, slow cogs, right direction etc.

Always keep interested in something.

Animal Communication

The best verification of transient harmony, especially in urban areas, is to have ones ideas and thoughts appraised or rejected by nature because the most indifferent opinion must be from the wild animals. It is good that their opinion has no direct links or dependence with Human habitation so that you may be confident of unbiased sincerity.

To give you the notion of what I mean I will give you some examples:

I will start with the birds, and yes it is true that all birds have different and recognisable song tunes, but it is within the song ranges of the birds that acceptance and denial reverberate. My favourite example is the common Wood Pigeon. They have very limited vocabulary, instead they have a resounding strength in judging right and wrong. Their most favoured songs are; 'whatever you do, whatever you do . . . 'which can change to; 'I know that you do, I know that you do . . . '. They are very good at distinguishing right from wrong, it is their forte. When they are pleased they purr like a cat and when they think that you have been clever they fly away clapping you with their wings, (sarcastically or not).

A different approach is taken by the Blackbird, whose talk is spontaneous and intellectual. They may not have a conversation with you, but they will automatically interact with your thought with either a linear word or short statement with a vocabulary as strong as ours.

Just sometimes there is a bird (not necessarily of a particular species) whose spirit is by all accounts an intellectual equal and whenever he/she arrives to talk I am stunned and respect it more for its mental status than any other single bird. It reminds me of The Archangel Gabriel.

There is one moment that I remember, though this was Gabriel as a jester and not of majesty. It was in the early days as my mind was opening to these revelations that I encountered him/her. Anyway it happened like this;

I heard a bird chirping. I looked around but could not see it. It was saying; 'Pick it up, pick it up.' To which I said 'What?' 'The red berry pick it up'. And sure enough there was a red berry. How obvious that this bird instructed me. 'It must be trying to help.' I thought. So I picked it up, at which point the bird chirped; 'Eat it, eat it'. This I did but on the first crunch the bird was laughing 'Now you're the Devil, now you're the Devil'. And it was laughing at me. I spat it out and washed my mouth with water.

This event proved to me that lending your whole life to enacting the entire transient order is some what foolish. Transience like all of life is not all holy and so should not be treated so. This is proof that we are not just existing we have wisdom and hindsight and a mind capable of making learned decisions, We have purpose. I think that what I learnt that day was about individuality and strength from God, who has made its possible for every one of us to be proud and unique.

Of course domestic animals such as dogs and cats are capable of learning their native tongue, not only to understand commands but actually to think in structured thought. And so when tamed can be good companions for doing so. Dogs will always bark as is their nature and this will generally be for attention or for protection of their domain and they do this not in structured sentences but as their instincts decree. They will though still say something and it is up to the transcendental to let them talk in the most appropriate way. This can be instinctive but dogs are good and have simple loyalty so there in lays what they may say. So a dog barking can and will respond to its surroundings and so if you are transcendental you will need certain management of its dialogue and you should expect that and no more or less.

There is another way of listening though and that is to learn what birds sing and assimilate that noise to one that renders it mute of non speak and that is a good thing. Like listening to something more beautiful than can be put into words. This is a wonderful place to be. And the more you practice and learn specific traits the better this world becomes. You can start with the Chiff-Chaff whose words simply repeat it name chiff-chaff but in varying order. And the Crow crows like a creaky barn door. This way not only do you get to hear the most amazing chorus but are also more able to distinguish which birds are around.

Transience in Art
'As a Painter'

As a painter I was always the conductor of my narrative and figural space. However I stumbled across what I considered to be another mind working on the canvas infiltrating unconsciously with relevance into my work. I first began to question figuration in what I thought was inert space i.e. sky grass or any flat area during my first year at University College. It took a while to understand what was going on, and I spent the rest of my time there experimenting with an idea of unconscious input. An involvement that was at least as prevalent in the figuration as I was. I slowly realised that the theory of my research lay with the Surrealist movement which occurred at the beginning of the twentieth century. While none of the previous painters had exposed quite as much unconscious narrative as I was getting, there were various texts that had been written with the same logic and there was a Surrealist Manifesto of 1924 by Andre Breton and some good talking by Clement Greenburg, probably the most famous art critic of his time, respected the world over by artists and collectors alike. It was this theory that provided the foundation for my work. Though it has to be said that my work seemed to be in an altogether more lush meadow, so the lack of tradition in this area was a shame. It meant that I had to form my own foundations which is an altogether more difficult thing.

With such an obvious outside force at work I gave the acquired figurative offering total respect and changed (or steered) very little. However after a while I came to realise that what was offered had about the same intrinsic validity as the response of the Superego, in other words there was room for transient error (though quite minimal). Because of this I exhibited some of my work, keen for it to be shown, before I had given it consideration which prevented me from fine tuning the content in order to balance the continual battle of right and wrong. And because of this oversight I fell short in the early stages when my method was in its infancy so the errors stood out and represented an inaccurate method swaying opinion to the idea of the figural 'coincidence' and the ever so renowned 'accident'. And so I believe my theory was subject to question and therefore regarded as well worked and not a genuine offering from an outside input.

There are possibilities as to where this unconscious input is from. The first option for me to explore is the Jungian theory of a 'Collective Unconscious'. Now the existence of a collective unconscious at first seems like a good idea. But when the realities of such a space are unravelled I think there will be a few sceptics. We are not talking about a subconscious space, that could be understood because if it were then we would know roughly its content as it would constitute things of a collective understanding of an institution or a subject (it would be like gossip). No we are talking of a pool of collective intelligence harboured by God. Which to some could be the most God like atheist's God. However this I feel would be naïve as the world is far to miraculous than that, I do believe in God and therefore believe him to

I Won't Do Wrong

harbour our collective thought. So am I somehow able to be a medium for this collective unconsciousness. I believe that I have found a door into this unconscious world. I believe it to be our fourth dimension. And I believe that voice hearing has its relevance here also. (Re ch Voice Hearing) There may be other doors into this unconscious world. It is an interesting and reasonably unexplored arena that may hold out hopes for the future.

Putting aside the collective unconscious, where else could this unconscious input come from? God of course is a real romantic contender. (everyone would like a direct line to our Lord.) But the outside input and probably the least romantic possibility is that I am being a medium for my own unconscious and am therefore working in a cellular manner, which if I believed I would probably stop painting. I feel that it is bigger and more complex than that. Of course one can never be one hundred percent sure, but with my theory of the 'Ultra World' where ones spirit may go (note that the spirit lives in the conscious world but also in the Ultra World flitting effortlessly between the two) the evidence starts to mount for the existence and tangibility of a fourth dimension. The Ultra World maybe acting as a stabiliser whilst the conscious mind is busy. All of this evidence leads me to believe in the Jungian pool of unconsciousness and ultimately the fourth dimension.

It is important to note that I paint through a method of automatism using colour and line randomly creating a pattern where there are no benefits from looking and analysing a work until 90% of the canvas is filled. That way I can be sure to have had no intellectual or actual recognition of any figural notation. So by just simply painting and covering the canvas where my only conscious input is creating a pattern I have no possible way of creating narrative. And so the figural narrative must have come from some where else. Perhaps from my own unconscious or the Jungian unconscious or maybe even higher power than that. Some of this theory suggests that if we can do nothing else then we can be transient. That way we can still allow for Gods destiny.

I wrote an essay in the second year of my degree course explaining how I theorised the progression and method of my 'automatic reflection of the unconscious' and how I learnt to paint automatically creating a pattern like building the perfect nest where they are different every time but the pattern remains the same and so my paintings can have the same pattern every time and yet allow for the catching of unconscious narrative. This allows for the most efficient extraction of unconscious figural narrative. Below is that essay which I have shortened and corrected any first draft inaccuracies.

Transience in Automatism

Painting is an all sensory involvement and as such can be a process of self discovery. Its process is one that can be therapeutic in explaining meanings in the confusion of all the inquisitive Human mind.

It seems evident that art can be as much about psychology as aesthetics and that the level of correctness in narrative within automatism can only be expressed fully when the medium (the artist) is in his most relaxed or distracted but confident state, thereby opening the door to the unconscious.

The reason for this belief comes from my study of works produced by using the Surrealist notion of automatism.

I Won't Do Wrong

If it was not my conscious self directing the picture, then surely it could be explained by theory. My findings showed that yes automatism was the source of my work and that it was a progression from the Surrealists and before them the Dadaists. But what was not evident in these past works was the huge figural unconscious input that I was getting. This therefore left my work unique in its abundant figural content in contrast to what previous painters were producing.

I studied the Jungian theory of the collective unconscious and combined it with the Freudian theory of consciousness. He states three levels of consciousness and I began to use this theory in explaining the manifestation of figural narrative that appeared so willingly, yet unannounced, onto my canvas.

Basic Freudian psychology states three levels of consciousness; the Id is a subconscious level of thought; the Ego is the part of the personality structure that deals with external reality and controls the energies of the Id.; While the Superego is one that records punishment and reward so that it comes to operate instinctively from past events. (This is a most important theology).

So the more practical experience one gets with painting with automatism the easier it is for the Superego to recognise a pattern that is most suited to transgressing unconscious thought. I believe that there is a pattern that can be laid down acting as the perfect medium for the reception of figuration much like a birds nest the figural representation will be different each time, though the nest quite similar.

The difference between subconscious and unconscious is most easily differentiated by the term I have used, called 'cutting'. An act of the unconscious is more likely to cut ones personal experience in transience as it may be foreign to what the artist knows. Of course it is still transient just from a different source. Where 'an act of the subconscious' is more likely to reinforce the act of the conscious. Having said that they are close together and when you get surprised by seeing something figural, that you have painted but not planned, it is much cherished and fun. It is the consistency of this relevant figural narrative that made me wonder what intellect was driving the figural input, both narrative and figural features appeared to be laid down next to each other confirming intelligence of some sort, which supports my theory of 'the more than accidental'. And herein lay my foundations.

I have come to believe that it is the subconscious that is the best way into the unconscious as they are close together. The question is when does the subconscious finish and the unconscious begin? It is because of this ambiguity that automatism is the perfect medium for accessing unconscious forces for the subconscious encourages the unconscious. This unconscious arena I determine is not a lunacy just a respective attribute of Jungian theology.

I can state that of the outside forces there are likely to be three; Firstly there is your own subconscious and possible unconscious (a result of the partially separated complimentary spirit which is able to work on its own within the Ultra World).; Secondly a collective unconscious (a derivative of many minds) and Thirdly the voice of God and a higher intelligence (a gift from a super conscious reality).

An interesting quote that supports my theory comes from Art and Illusion.

'To sketch . . . is to transfer ideas from the mind to paper . . . to blot is to make varied forms . . . from which ideas are presented to the mind . . . To sketch is to delineate ideas; blotting suggests them.' Page 157, Art and Illusion 1959.

The subtlety in the appearance of image through the blotting method is one that encourages me as an artist, and is the consequence of low level, subconscious or unconscious origin a gift or an accident or both! I am however ruling out the accident as my theory suggests.

I must state that I am always fighting the line of wrong and right and that any figuration must be viewed as dispensable though the most fun occurs when the canvas is bursting with figural narrative where overlaying images lay themselves onto the work causing the viewer an aesthetic challenge.

So yes, I may have no idea what the painting will be before its construction but oppositely I also know that it will be, in the end, because of my faith, a battle where right prevails over wrong.

Transient Error

> Father eternal, giver of light and grace,
> we have sinned against you and against our neighbour,
> in what we have thought,
> and in what we have said and done,
> and through our own deliberate fault
> We have wounded your love
> and marred your image in us.
> We are sorry and ashamed,
> and repent of all our sins,
> For the sake of your son Jesus Christ, who died for us,
> forgive us all that is past;
> and lead us out from darkness
> to walk as children of the light.
> Amen

This prayer helps to explain the fragility of the Human mind and the remorse that we must show to keep in accordance with all that is good and the place where we know we should be. This is possible through Jesus, for he has given God understanding of our suffering to his father through his life and his crucifixion. Jesus has allowed us compassion and intellectual solace. In a world that strives for perfection of liberty, we may through the rationalisation of our own inability to be perfect recompense for our

I Won't Do Wrong

inadequacies by simple prayer through Jesus who knows us. This simple cleansing can be done because Jesus has flattened the path and so without him life would be empty but with him life can be full.

Transient error is the result of confusion, stress or illness. The point to emphasise is that we have been given freedom of thought by God and we must not fail his premise that we are capable of ruling life and be respectful and responsive to change and intellect inside and outside of our own control. Our transient world should be filled with likeminded respect. We must remember though that the world is like a ship and we the crew are responsible for negotiating the waters some of which are calm but some are much rougher. We are most able to cope with these waters, but it will take concentration. For if you think that every thought may be an action, like a turn on the tiller, you may see how easy it can be to lose ones way. There will be times when you miss the best thought, not that you may have chosen a wrong one, just not the best and you will recognise this as it is an example of transient error. It is for this reason (which seems as important as any other) that religion and communication with God can be fundamental in captaining our ships correctly. It can be as simple as recharging the batteries or filing with diesel. We must be gracious to our selves in this way which is why I have said that ninety-nine percent of cognitive accuracy is pretty good going.(re ch. Ninety-Nine Percent). And so the above prayer has some meaning for it indicates that we are aware of our weakness' so that God and Jesus can restore us so that we may keep our faith.

I would say that transient error is the worst thing about being transient for 'if all the worlds a stage' then we must be directing our thought twenty-four seven. Mohamed undertook this responsibility by demanding that he prayed five times a day, Jesus did so by offering himself as a messiah after an amazing journey during which time he taught with authority by serving his father our Lord. Everyone is entitled to go and pray in the traditional way (as I do some times) and if you believe in the power of prayer, in a transcendental way, why not be prepared to pray all the time. We are capable of this and most people probably do. What I mean by this is simply thinking well of people. I take the stance that my sincerity is enough to effect good prayer whenever and wherever my instinct directs. Hence the best way to pray in my experience is 'when you feel the impulse to do so or all the time which can only be done if you feel that it is in your nature. To pray all the time sounds impossible but what I mean is simply to navigate your thought in the best possible way which is something that you probably already do but be conscious of your captaincy because that in my book is good prayer. A person can encourage good prayer for what ever they wish at a time when the Leigh lines are closest, a time where the transient energy is weakest between the lines and the prayer therefore most effective. This is a new arena of prayer that can bring hope and peace and a sense of duty. The only tumbling stone is transient error which can make you look wrong. Not all thought is played out on non speak but when ever transient error does, it is likely to stand out as it ruffles the most feathers which is because it is wrong. It stems from the reality that in ones thought there is no room for tumbleweed (or at least very rarely) . . . point being that to want to say nothing often is not an option. Herein lays the confusion. Continuous thought is something that can of course be mastered. There will be no reason for causing a transient error. It is simply inherent in mankind. The mind is simply programmed to be cognitively active ninety-nine percent of the time. So if there is error it will not be due to vengeance or greed but will be the result of a tired mind. This point is clear, there is rarely any truth or reason behind such an error (Hence its name). All you have to do is play something nice by which I mean that you will have to learn to conduct a symphony. Don't get stuck on your error. Be decisive and think what it is you want to be thinking and think of it. It is fundamentally easy. It is the gradual accumulation of the tiredness of an active mind that can cause error. We all know that good thought is easy. It will be the duration of continual prayer (sincere thought) that you may stumble on, but don't worry God is understanding and forgiving and a friend. It is relatively easy (apart from its difficult starting pattern in the case of someone being locked out). For some it can be a steep learning curve but perservere. Man can tackle most things and work out almost anything (which is his gift). So I believe hope springs eternal. Give yourself a good start and begin to question the ways of the world and the ways of God. This should be enough to let you see God's destiny and give you a chance of being a part of it.

As a famous band once said 'your best is good enough' no one can expect anything more!

In accordance with the above script, by which I mean learning the ways of God and seeing his destiny, I will introduce a new idea one of conning transient response into action, the idea is of a non prayer which I term **'Mistransubstantiation'**. This term is the worst form of transubstantiation. It is like a non prayer that fools transience into action. The best example of this is voodoo.

Voodoo encourages the idea that the consumption of animal parts will affect healing by using the rarity of the intrinsic component and the essence of the magnificence of the animal being used. By doing this they try to con a transient response, one that would not be offered if the truth was known. The true prayer would be to ritualise a ceremony where the spirit of the animal be rejoiced and prayer affected by asking for the continuation of its life.

It has its less potent examples like breathing smoke through a cigarette whilst sucking in someone else's energy (an example I have taken from a time in hospital). I found it better to take energy from feet instead, as to say you have good feet which is actually something good. So Mistransubstantiation is to be avoided and transient error to be minimised. Both are more likely to occur whilst tired.

Another form of transient error is that of morphing speak and non speak. It is possible to correct converse to say something other than that which was said by using the way words hang in the air. Now this is a tool for the transient if something requires alteration. This of course only holds water if sincerely directed. This is the positive side of the coin as the transient may also change things that he would not like to by simply mishearing, which may transgress error.

We know that the Superego reacts instinctively and that error on the Superego is therefore much more of an upset. Remember that it is possible to talk in tongues. So for the transcendental television watcher listen to what is being said with real words as well as the Superego as this will concentrate the transient mind back into the situation actually. Listen to the reading as a whole and if you are simply not interested turn over. If however you

I Won't Do Wrong

feel tarnished by transient error perservere and you will be rewarded for expressing distaste and showing a determined mind as what you meant to say should transgress, which is admirable because God will always encourage love and the act of perseverance is an act of faith.

I have been working on a theory that I am only just permitting myself to write. It is transient error of the supernatural. The idea that Leigh lines sometimes have points where two or more may be very close together which may and I repeat may be subject to transient error due to their importance. A time where the exact opposite of correctness occurs with an apparent lack of human transient involvement. One could say that it is still human error but closer to home but I detract this because the skill and brilliance of individuals has taught me to. The next question 'Is anyone to blame' or can there just be freak accidents of perfect destruction something that would be impossible to recreate even through endeavour. You may say no and I might agree. But before moving on it is important to look at this through Jungian eyes and the idea of a collective unconscious. Is it right to blame this lesser than holy culprit? It certainly bears better than to blame God, though God maybe its harbourer. So how complex is Gods role and how interactive can he be? Well he is interactive with us and our transience and with out him we would all be lost because he acts on the process of things working and by doing so offers information, advice and direction. He is considering and caring and spontaneous and it is this point that refers me toward transient error. There is a place where very little transient energy is required to change Leigh lines (as they at some points come very close together), essentially these are easy mistakes with huge consequences.

Is God apparently wrong in spontaneity sometimes given that his source of involvement could be from the Ultra World as well as from the Physical World where there exists 'folly' that could be confusing. Does something guide his spontaneity at a tangent sometimes? Well with split second decisions of emotion and action, it sounds like an easy error to make. If this is the case then it should be up to us to create the best unconscious as possible. This shows us how important having correct thought paths are. I suppose what I am questioning is the idea that if we all thought better by considering thought to be prayer would the world be a physically better place?

There is an alternative though, God may simply need these particular people in heaven, in order to help the other side with importance, this I guess we will all find out some day.

Transcending Time

This chapter investigates transience that may appear to transcend time. The best example comes from the superego's of those on television. It is true that because the 'man' (on TV) is talking and that we are listening he has his links with the present. The superego is a trait of the present and will therefore conduct itself afresh every time, whether it be from the same piece of music or a news report or whatever happens to be repeated. The superego will always appear afresh whenever watched though there may be traits that will tend to stay the same. So I can confirm that you are not transcending time.

I have also noticed that even with pre-recorded footage the 'man' will be looking at the transcendental no matter where in the room he is. I can also confirm that the transient may through will power let those eyes focus on someone else though this is quite a hard trick.

I think that I have touched upon the idea that (again with pre-recorded viewing) a dialogue (of the Superego) can be relevantly different on each view where it is being real to the present. I repeat; this is not transcending time. I like to put this Superego response in the same field as the partially separated spirit that may conduct on anything thought or said anywhere any time. So the fact that it is in the past does not stop the viewing from being in the present and likewise the 'man' is therefore also in this respect in the present.

Time for me is the only constant.

Association

This chapter offers a piece of advice which is very easy to use. It is common for the Human mind to put things together, things that may be similar or have a direct or relative link in some way (association). This trait can be put to good use in personal conduct as in Cognitive Mental Practice. Ultimately you may choose your line of thought and say what you think is interestingly connected. Use your spontaneity by acknowledging good relevant thought, though you needn't say everything that you know on a subject (re ch. Situation Actually). This instinctive connection of subject is one of our best traits. It shows intellect and an ability to think outside of the box allowing us to solve problems and construct marvellous things. So with this in mind it only makes sense to utilise this Human gift for our social wellbeing as well as for our practical matters.

The opposite is also true, in that you may find a link that is not appropriate, but like I said you don't have to say everything you know or think (re ch Situation Actually). Such unnecessary thought if transgressed would come under the title 'transient error'. What I am saying is utilise this Human trait. Don't hide from it because that would be denying some of your existence, work with it and you will become friends.

By not ignoring this psychology but embracing it paranoia can be averted. I can liken this to the way that we see God (re chapter Seeing God). In a nut shell if you remain

I Won't Do Wrong

positive and walk over bad thought with strength you will learn to do it instinctively (Super Ego). You will see better and feel better. All this can be done by applying association as a tool and not as a trap. So think good and you will see good and associate well and you will work well.

Book 3

Theories

Voice Hearing

This has been a phenomenon for centuries and I feel that I am up to date with what people experience. Having first being aware of 'heard voices', at the age of nineteen, when I experienced my first breakdown (notably cannabis made me worse). It became obvious to me after a while that the dialogue I was receipting was sporadic and unlikely. The truth remained though that there was more than one voice from more than one person and that they were not of a holy order.

I did not appreciate at the time that I was a most transcendental person and that it was my intrinsic strength that was conducting a Spirit World that was not being true to life. I found this extremely confusing, and I was probably seriously confusing it for others.

I have learnt from then on, up to the age of thirty (when I solved the voice hearing equation completely), the real potential for the Spirit World. In that I have noticed two different arenas that the spirit flits between, one the Physical World the other the Ultra World. The arena encompassed by the Spirit World the one I call 'The Ultra World' operates outside of the talkers conscious and therefore you must accept the existence of folly. The other arena allows for the state of Mentelepathy and is the act of one mind talking to another in the Physical World.

The Spirit World therefore harbours a real importance of 'Mentelepathy' which is the connection of one mind meeting another as real entities recognised and conducted by the conscious of both transients (a form of long distance telepathy).

So the Spirit World exists, in both the Ultra World and the Physical World and Mentelepathy is a construct of the Physical World. But a spirit in the Ultra World may also be heard but only truly to the respondent (of the Physical World) because the spirit of the other is out of his/hers consciousness and in the Ultra World but still being operative. Importantly it still offers a true 'response possibility' (potential folly). The trick is that the spirit in the Ultra World doesn't know where it is, so it is all real to him/her but unreal to any real life scenario.

It is especially important for strong transients to ignore at their will its ramblings. I have found that to drink a gallon of it leads clear to error, but to sip a tea spoon of it when ever you want is enriching. I also find that to rest when one is stressed or has done a lot of concentrated activity is very good for rerouting ones Zen. Whereby allowing some time to catch up (with transient connections) reduces urgency in them by the calming nature of rational spirit response.

What my theory entails is the concept that along with our conscious mind, body and soul we come armed with a complementary spirit which is only partially connected to the body and mind physical. And I call the world that encompasses the spirits existence the 'Spirit World'. The Spirit World lives in two arenas the 'Ultra World' and the 'Conscious Spirit World' (in our conscious thought). The existence of the 'Ultra World' is paramount to my theory and was I believe first explained by Jung and he called it the 'Collective Unconscious'. The spirit flits effortlessly between the two worlds and because it does so it causes confusion. The other arena the 'Conscious Spirit World' allows true converse between two transient minds and I call this 'Mentelepathy'. So there is a place in our lives where our spirits can be united with our conscious minds and when two people are in this state a true form of trans telepathy may occur; 'Mentelepathy'. There is also a place where the spirit lives in our unconscious world. And because our conscious mind is intrinsically unaware of its proceedings folly is easily made; This unconscious world I call the 'Ultra World' but believe it first appearing as the Jungian Collective Unconscious.

An interesting point to make here is: Where does God appear in this complex state of transverse? Voice hearing is an inexact science. God we know responds to the physical otherwise we would not know him. (Re; Transient Response). However is it not possible that God responds also to our 'collective unconscious'? If so then to offer him folly must be wrong therefore we must respect our part in the Ultra world. Will good thought make Gods life easier?

Transcendental voice hearers have the strength to listen to voices but more importantly they have the strength to influence them (in the same way they may influence non speak) which is why transcendental voice hearing is somewhat of an art form. My theory states that a Retranscendental person may hear voices without the ability to change them. I have coined the term Retranscendental to explain a different intrinsic transient strength. A Retranscendental person may be very aware of the operations of transience but lacks the ability to change things. This is a very good mind for observation and assessment.

It is for this reason, among others, that I have written chapter 'Opt Out' which is such an important notion because these are tools of progress not of regress. Because of this I say drink in teaspoons not of pints, this will allow a more accurate analysis of the spirit world.

What is folly?

Folly, in this case, represents a direction of narrative that may be alien to the emitters knowledge, the spirit that is in the 'Ultra World' may be drawn into a topic that is neither relevant nor real, but it will be an honest response to the persons personality and honour making the converse seem very real. This is folly because out here in the physical world it offers no bearing.

I have experienced folly at its most obvious when I was nineteen I was unconsciously changing and inventing whole scenarios, where people were in pain and such like. I did however always see these voice as my friends and not of God so from then on I have tried to explain, where I can, the how's where's and why's of psychosis/schizophrenia in order to prevent preventable instances. Education can prevent needless crime. Hence my organising this the book that I originally wrote for my own analysis and therapy.

So the spirit and the conscious are somewhat separate but can perfectly join when the conscious of both minds determine and it is at this stage that Mentelepathy can take place. But that it is very hard to determine these times exactly (as the spirits in the Ultra World will sound the same). The spirit will however live and conduct its existence by toing and frowing from the Physical to the Ultra World and because of their constant reconnection one keeps ones Zen and harmony with the world in the long run. It is up to us to decide with reflection and reservation what is actually going on.

I Won't Do Wrong

One thing is clear though; the person may not understand all that the spirits have said and seen whilst you are working (because the spirit will be in the Ultra World). After all we can't be talking to ourselves all the time, which is why it is good to take five minutes out to realign and unite your spirit if you need to; for the purpose of Zen. This has its links with praying whenever you think appropriate, it can be difficult but also easy. Essentially all it means is be true to your thought as much as possible; prayer is reliant on sincerity of thought and if you have this already then that is your prayer. To underline this theory; the link between the mind and the spirit (of the same person) is considerably fractured and that there is a part of our spirit and therefore personality able to drift into an unconscious arena where its separation is reflected in the folly produced which may be picked up by someone else.

If this is so then it would go a long way into explaining why schizophrenia has not been 'breeded out' through natural selection because voice hearing is intrinsic in the Human make up but has up to now not been recognised. It is real to the physical consciousness, if you know how to filter out the folly which is also real but only to the spirit world and therefore folly in the Physical World. One must therefore drink in teaspoons and not in pints. What I must make clear is that the voices that I hear are not of a divine nature. You wouldn't run under a bus if your mate told you to, so don't if your transient mate tells you to either.

One of the most compelling aspects of voice hearing, is their synonymous nature; (i.e. they can be heard by more than one person at the same time). Now scientifically speaking that is an important observation. It not only helps to confirm their existence but also helps toward pin pointing their origin. The voices appear to hang in the air (or at least are accessible on a larger than personal wavelength) so that everyone near can hear. As two radios pick up the same frequency so maybe two heads do in a similar manner. This seems most likely as they can not be picked up on hi tech recording equipment. In short the idea of coincidence and randomness are ruled out in my mind, because of their synonymous nature convinces me that it is more than just one mind hallucinating. This opens up the playing field considerably.

I feel that I am missing a beat and it is not a good one. Now there is a chance that like converse in the real world insults may be brandished about, and unlike the real world they are not easy to prevent, but the more you persevere the easier it will be. If this is a problem then you must intellectualise and work out why you like someone and work out social stand points etc. Remember though this arena is full of folly so try not to concern yourself with it too deeply. This in itself will help.

So there is considerable room for error and folly so to try and express the truth in this thick purple soup could be confusing. For the purpose of explaining the validity of voices I have categorised the 'Voices Of The Mind' into three different arenas that together explain voice hearing as I see it. These are listed below.

Firstly; There are the voices that remain correct. These are generally of a rudimentary nature about things that are of no great surprise, things that are OK. These voices are usually someone you speak to regularly (tea spoon stuff). Strangely though this converse is not usually Mentelepathical, it is simply a spiritual connection from physical to spirit. This

I Won't Do Wrong

can be achieved because the spirit is complementary to the physical and will generally give the same response.

Secondly; There are the changed voices that offer folly. And there are two types of these.

A. there is the folly of a Mentelepathical respondent who's concentration may have lapsed or who may have lost interest or just getting it wrong for no particular reason.

B. there is the folly that is encountered when a strong mind is searching in a worried manner and has thus created a whole untrue scenario. It appears that this type of folly needs to be proved wrong by the physical. In other words evidence that an event has clearly not occurred and this requires whatever physical evidence may be necessary. In this instance the folly occurs because the spirit is capable of entering the Ultra World where it acts as it would in the Physical World but without the real knowledge of the mind Physical and so the spirit is capable of formulating its own identity, if only for a while. It is important to explain that it seems possible for the worried and strong transient to keep peoples spirits in the Ultra World which will increase their separate identities and escalate the folly.

It is also possible for the spirit to announce itself in front of both respondents. This is known to me because it comes as a surprise to both transmitter and receptor who are both in ear shot of each other. 'That wasn't my voice, I didn't think that' categorically. Which encourages the theory that the voices heard are a construct of an unconscious mind. It is possible that the transient may be compartmentalising it out of the Jungian pool of collective unconsciousness However I do feel that if there is a state of hallucination that this is where it is, because in my opinion if hallucination is evident anywhere then it is here which leads me to the idea that one may hallucinate and construct something real.

So the idea that the Spirit World can be manipulated into folly by a strong transient mind is science fact. If the strongest transient mind has its full sincerity behind something it would occur as truth to the Spirit World where more often than not he will be creating a thick purple soup of his own. He will not realise that because his sincerity is true and as I have been promoting sincere thought as active prayer so the folly continues. This is a case most vulnerable to the confusion as I have talked about above second (B.) It is most likely to be delusion for the reasons that I have discussed above which is most unfortunate as most people won't get the physical evidence brought before them and so the psychosis continues. So although its fact is wrong its sincerity is right and so there is the loop hole. The Spirit World may be unaware of folly and it will be accepted by the Ultra World as truth.

Thirdly ; There may be someone who is real to the physical offering Mentelapathical response but who is deliberately causing folly as an act of malice or he may simply being wrong or ill.

Importantly; those who have a highly transcendental mind must accept that to block out the voices (beyond the teaspoon analogy) is a recommended course of action. Why? Because of the intrinsic ability to control everything that is transient makes anything worthwhile very hard to do. However the acknowledgement of their being is paramount for success. (There is no need to be locked out for that is a rocky road). And yes sometimes it is impossible not to 'tune in', this is the time to lend an ear and be competent.(re 'Opt Out' in order to experience voices Retranscendentaly).

I Won't Do Wrong

It is possible that you may be dealing with complex issues and the required concentration may draw in a transient with specific knowledge. Accept this as advice. It all helps, it can be that good especially if you know a few scholars.

We know that voices may be heard synonymously, that is by more than one person, but this is not to say that there are no more than one spirit converse happening at once. Indeed there are possibilities for many more. In fact I would be very surprised if there was only room for one field or one wavelength for transient talking.

Below I have answered some of the most common questions in relation to voice hearing and the effect they can have on a person.

Is it somewhere that you can find a friend or soul mate? Probably.

Is it somewhere that can make you ill? Yes but this can be remedied through education or treatment.

Is it somewhere that may confuse you and prevent you living normally and leave you in a dangerous state of mind? Yes but neglecting your own needs is most common.

Is it something that can be remedied with education? Yes many people would be happier with the knowledge that voice hearing can simply be a Human trait and that with the right knowledge is manageable with Gods support.

Is it possible to conduct converse better with medication? Yes definitely but only if you experience psychosis or prolonged misunderstandings.

One more thing that I would like to emphasise is that the louder and clearer the voice the more likely it is to be Mentelepathical.

It is important at this stage to separate the misinterpretation of external noise. For example the television downstairs. This is a separate area of voice hearing because it is based on real background noise. I have understood the cunning manner in which whole conversations can be heard but as to whether this is linked to some sort of spiritual connection I am not sure. I would suggest that it is definitely a manifestation of the mind which intrinsically is always looking for patterns. However, it is clear that 'no one ever heard any good from listening in'. The solidity of the audio structure and the validity of heard converse leads me to wonder whether this is another string to the Ultra Worlds bow. Another medium for the unconscious to project its presence And with this knowledge I am excited. The folly that comes with the Ultra World is prevalent and probably more active in this type of voice hearing so the potential for delusion / folly again is high. Very high.

In Addition To Previous Text

I find it necessary to add a little of my own understanding of spiritual guidance. It is clear that the source of this is everything we understand in our selves and our surroundings. The muscle twitches for example can create a personal language of converse, and that they come from three sources;

Firstly; semi-subconscious
Secondly; subconscious
Thirdly; unconscious or outside transient force.

I Won't Do Wrong

If this is new then this may be a first understanding of God, (also listen out for the TV creaking in fact anything that comes the transient way.)

Warning

This chapter comes with a warning : The amount of folly even if very little reduces the validity of anything heard and so the validity of Mentelepathy is reduced. Be wise but do nothing with haste and always respect the surprise of folly's proof. In other words by being prepared to be wrong actually makes you more right.

Ninety-Nine Percent

I have written this chapter in order to put forward an understanding of the fragility of the Human mind and the nature of its function.

The truth is that it can require a huge input by the responder to account for multiple transient Leigh lines. After all you can only have one conversation at a time. A Leigh line is like a groove and a path set out before you. A path that is already laid. It is in essence the direction of your life and its destiny but it can change and probably will do so as you find new things to add and change its direction. One's Leigh line may change and this may occur when other Leigh lines come close to your own which can be a choice or a destiny. Trying to occupy two Leigh lines at a time is like trying to conduct two conversations at the same time, it is not an asset that us Humans are very gifted at. An example of this is trying to listen to the church bells in a transient manner whilst having a conversation with your neighbour at the same time. And so some error will inevitably be expected. But this is where faith is important, because if you have faith then God will carry you through any confusion, God will do his bit for you so don't worry too much.

The Human mind is properly armed to deal with confusion, but we are not machines. Ironically however like machines we can break down though generally if properly looked after one does not expect this to happen too often.

And so 99% cognitive accuracy is a pretty good result. What I am trying to say is try not to worry too much about a slight error if you do so then you could increase the error which would be like making a mountain out of a mole hill. Every car gets a flat tyre occasionally and we don't let it get us down. We should act similarly, simple problem simple result, because not to do so would be to over react and the stress of this could magnify wrong doing and lead unnecessarily to paranoia. Confidence with God and Jesus as your best ally, the captain of the team, makes it possible to live well.

Vulnerability is one feature of Humanity and we cannot therefore expect to 'win every battle'. And so some adverse reaction to a problem through stress or tiredness may be an instinctive response, which is quite normal. Even the best in the world (and you may become one of these) cannot deny the complexity of the power bestowed to one person by God, who has made us in reflection of himself and thus giving us the power of free thought and action, because he knows and trusts us.

Ninety-nine percent freedom from error is a reasonable expectation and an achievable target. If it were not, life would be less meaningful with no need for compassion or intellect and that would be a darker world and a less important existence. So we are not alone. Faith and transience are with us also.

One must always respect the fragility of the Human condition and its mortality but with a few basic rules, and with God and Jesus' strength a kind heart will win the day and we may then be strong and our own representatives on Earth as it is in Heaven hopefully.

Opt Out

This is one of the hardest skills that a transcendental will need to master. It is achieved only by the notion that others have more important transience than to judge or to be judged by you. Confidence is paramount and this can only be achieved through good experiences and successes, but alas it still takes nerves to initially pass on non speak responsibility. It is hard putting your faith in an unproven arena because you know the buck stops with you. So sometimes you have to be dominant and direct. I promise this will get easier. I have already stated that this requires faith and not only in people but also with God who is forgiving beyond what you would expect, for he has confidence that love will transgress the truth.

I must make clear that the term 'Opt Out' means to allow others to conduct their own non speak essentially by withdrawing your transient mind. It is so intrinsic though that this can be hard to do. Most people would do this automatically and the only real stress comes from those who are learning it for the first time and who have high transience. However this is not to say that you should forget your own responsibility not only transiently but as being an equal member of society. You must direct all the necessary intervention needed to uphold politeness and courtesy but you must also have faith in others. I have used the term cutting before (which I primarily learnt from painting automatically). Well Opting Out is basically allowing the

I Won't Do Wrong

world to go by without transient cutting. Basically if you can stop cutting and changing Leigh lines that are perfectly good already you will find life much richer and easier. Not to do so would be to over burden your self. So Opting Out is essential for you to maintain life that is not only hard enough already but rewarding enough too. After all why change the direction of a Leigh line if it is already going in the right direction?

Arguably the hardest part of Opting Out is putting down the phone. By which I mean disconnecting with converse. This can be an awkward and sticky trap that is basically one being over involved and being unable to disconnect with a converse after it has finished. There are probably many remedies for this but I find that there are three which are pretty effective allowing you a good exit from an over transient connection.

Firstly via assimilation: This is the idea of thinking about something positive (usually connected in some way to the transient converse). This will allow your mind to wonder somewhere else and free up the other conversers mind to their own thought. This should lead you naturally out of converse.

The second remedy is distraction simply to think of those who you love. 'Being strong for others'. Because family and friends should be top of anyone's list. And try not to worry about the other person because strength and faith are the masters of this scenario. God helps the transgression as he does with most things but what will teach you the most is 'cognitive competence' where by remembering what is important to you and deciding what it is that you actually want to think and then think of it. This will steer your ship in the best possible way.

For the confidence that you require, build on small successes, as these will accumulate and, if maintained, will grow into larger successes. If the foundations are good and correct and it is sweet at the start then it will be sweeter at the end.

The Third method is to embrace the converse and continue it but through the Ultra World. Why? Because the Ultra World distances you from the physical and allows for prayer which will detract from any real time stress. This could be done just for a bit until you wonder on to your next point of interest (which should come soon). I got this idea through the church bells, when I noticed that I could still hear them even when out of hearing range. And because there is this separation, and connection, (like a semi conductor) both parties are able to use this attribute to reveal a seamless transmission between transient paths.

The Dying of the Demi-God

This sounds like a loss of some sort. On the contrary however it is a release of an isolation that if not discovered sets you on your own. It is a realisation of mortality and the start of service to God. It is a time when the transcendental renounces his audible world from his personal and selfish control where before his naivety made the slog of the demi-god the only path. Relinquishing his majesty through the insight of a divine source or larger outside force, (which is his new found respect for his transient world), will capture his imagination and he will be inspired. He must stop and notice because the importance of the recognition of the involvement of other intellectual transience's is essential for finding God and ones place in his world. Like an epiphany he may see God for the first time which will in turn relieve a hundred weight from his shoulders. This new insight may be a worry initially but the journey is worth taking. The transient on entering this new world may have a rocky start. There will be a lot of reconsidering and experimentation with transience in order to find the truth of life and therefore the validity of one's actions. So there is a likely hood that the respondent may withdraw from life a bit, when he realises that the world is bigger than he ever could have imagined. He may scan back to reassess situations that he may until now never have realised the weight of actions on his mind and the consequent response in transience. There is the notion that a locked out and self perpetuating respondent will not see his own folly but will cut into transience for his own selfish though naive needs. In a sense this chapter has links with 'Opt Out' as he/she will have to Opt Out of their Ultra Ego that may reveal its self as not being his 'best friend'. In a sense he/she will be opting out of bad behaviour as a larger more towering member of consciousness enters into his existence and illuminates his folly. A part of the demi-god allows and even thrives on cutting into transience for entertainment (which is in its self not bad after all spontaneity is the birth place of humour) but also there is the propensity for frivolous behaviour by which I mean placing a low level of importance on things that should be high in mind. Living without God is much more meaningless. This behaviour, when recognised as the doings of the demi-god, will be tossed aside and the diminishment of this naivety will progress.

Life for a while may become daunting.

One has now become a part of an equal world where the importance of narrative, thought and spontaneity, from a new collective understanding, seems perfectly clear. It is a place where transcendental intervention will become so much more personal and logical. It is a starting point and you may now build for the future.

The joy of being a part of this transient world is enough to realise the enormity of being in part responsible for not being so before. Because though unrealised there is a definite blindness to this part of the world which needs only your will to offer yourself to God to see. There are many reasons why this light cannot be seen by some and from experience I think that most of all it is the unjustifiable nature of ones own predicament leading to an unavoidable lack of faith.

I Won't Do Wrong

However unhappy you may have been, it is intrinsic to life, and the resultant feeling of acceptance and participation pushes any other path to one side.

It is important to stress that those who have been locked out, by which I mean people who do not understand themselves enough to understand transient forces, may never have considered the notion of the demi-god let alone the dying of it. Being locked out through ones own inability to accept the truth will be enough to also block out the transient world. This leads to a total blindness to everything transient. By this stage the whole transient world will need to be reconstructed as truth by the individual, which is what I have achieved and why I have written this book and why I wish others to read it also. What I hope to encourage is an awareness of the advantages of the transient world and the openness of many roads that lead from it in comparison to the lonely narrow road, which one may be on for as long as it takes for the blindness to go and the light to be seen.

I feel it important to emphasise that while any protocolic operations may prevent one from seeing properly as a youngster some ground should be made during his/her teenage years depending on the severity of circumstance. If ground is not made and he/she turns to drink and or drugs he/she will be continuing the process of diversion through the escapism of their life style. They will then be self medicating in order for their lives to make sense, effectively keeping themselves locked out. If this happens then they will have to learn the ways of his/her transient world when their predicament decries, which is much harder.

Talking In Tongues

This is a similar experience to that of 'reading between the lines'. It is a situation where the actual voice projection becomes detached from what becomes understood from the conversation. It is when people are talking via their super ego's and where the actual spoken word, is or seems, irrelevant even not rememberable. So it is where peoples minds are talking (via the super ego) and it is the continuation of super ego response that conducts the direction of converse. So much so that the actual spoken words are forgotten and yet continued automatically to form a converse that is strictly of the super ego.

This is a vary rare occurrence and is spooky but intellectual. You may never witness this but it is there somewhere.

The Role of The Dream

I can only skim the surface of explaining 'the dream' and its whys and wherefores but I do feel that can offer some possible answers to some of the transient connections that seem to fill this space.

As you know I am a great believer in the Ultra World (Jungian collective unconscious) and so it would stand that I believe there is more involvement than simple imagination at work. I always feel surprised by detail in dreams, detail that at the time (whilst asleep) seem only curious. For example the colour of a car or the numbers and letters of its registration plate or the price of something. I believe that numbers have a certain affiliation with philosophical meaning and therefore have a specific relationship to the individual, though there are some more concrete certainties with stronger superstitious foundations that are less personal. It is the fact that numbers and letters do have a psychological impact that gives us more insight into our dreams. Not only is this wonderfully personal, it also goes to prove that there is a larger than personal intellect at work.

So what is at work? Well I can only guess at this and there are a few obvious starting places, The Holy Spirit, The Ultra World or simply our Imagination helped on with a bit of trans telepathy.

I consider the Holy Spirit and the Ultra World to be working along side each other, with the Holy Spirit keeping check on the Ultra World and God keeping check on the

Holy Spirit, which may be the spirit of Jesus (if not then very akin to his).

Imagination with a bit of external involuntary trans telepathy as both responders may be asleep, is a contender but in my view lags well behind the other two. It is true that this may have an impact after all the fourth dimension affects us while awake.

No I think that the Ultra World is more of a warehouse that busily orders and files away and sends stuff out, which might be relevant for the dream and probably is but the specific details would I believe come from the Holy Spirit.

An interesting part of the dream is its ability to be real, you do after all believe them at the time. So I shall put forward an idea that bears relevance for this book, which is memory. Do dreams give you false memory, in other word can you confuse dreams for actual events. Yes is the answer but only from your long term memory. Effectively you may have a dream and forget it and then have it again forget that it was a dream after many years, because at the time of the dream you should already have it installed in the memory. However there are cases of deja vu. But lightning can strike twice so you may already have had the same dream before and this might confuse your long term memory into thinking that the dream has come from physical past and not dream past.

Dreams from the past especially in childhood are most likely to infiltrate your long term memory of the physical because at a young age everything is new and so dreams may fit into the same category of visual memory.

One thing that I should say is that although the dream is in many ways, you are in control of how you respond to

I Won't Do Wrong

it. It is a bit like 'Seeing God' (Re Ch.) If you think well you will represent yourself better in your dream.

It is pretty unlikely that you remember all your dreams and I am quite sure that you are not supposed to, but if you wish to remember you are more likely to remember in the evening when you may get a spontaneous pulse of memory. You may then start to piece your dream together. It is true though that this feeling of knowing that you know and then forgetting what it is that you nearly remembered until all you remember is the feeling that you nearly remembered. This is both frustrating and curious.

However what will remain illuminating to me is the detail in the dream that is specific even more so than your own intellect would have constructed, and is of a nature that you wouldn't have expected. It is for these reasons, that have led me to think that there is a narrator and that it is not you or me. So the conclusion that I have made is that the narrator is likely to be the Ultra World with the aid of the Holy Spirit.

It is possible that this outside input could come from a parallel universe, like Heaven, but the closest transient link to us is the Holy Spirit and the Ultra World which construct the fourth dimension. I also believe that these two are reliant on each other and our closest path to God who I believe harbours their workings.

So now I understand the dream what role does it play in our lives? This area is quite well intellectualised by Freud and the philosophers so I shall only say a few words. Guidance. Reassurance. Notification. Warning. Settling

Generally a dream is a reflection of what are our present worries or elations are and a place where your mind is busy problem solving, reacting and acting. And where on a subconscious level Zen is being made through the rebalancing of ones mental energy. And this is probably the most important role for the dream 'Settling' creating harmonies and levelling the ground for the next day.

The Placebo Effect

The theory behind this idea is that prayer works via positive mental thought.

To explain; The placebo is a tablet that contains no medical properties and is given to half of the patients whilst the other half have nothing.

The results from such a survey show that those on the placebo tablet did better than those who took nothing. (i.e. neither placebo nor test drug).

Why?

The simple answer must be that prayer works. Prayer must then be considered as an important tool. And there is no point having a tool that you never use. So the question must be; How can we use this tool? The obvious strategy must be through religious endeavour and the act of prayer. This in itself however may not be the most efficient way to use this new tool. We must consider the notion that I have used before where by there is a certain destiny line for everything and the course that you are on is called your leigh line. And we must recognise that transient response comes more easily when two leigh lines come close together. So this is when the placebo (prayer) should be undertaken as, transcendentally it may have more impact. Obviously the best prayers are prayed with belief that sincerity may make a difference (as the placebo test has shown us), for God will act and respond to prayer. So what I am saying is that there are strictly two types of prayer. Firstly there is the conventional religious path where one prays to God through Jesus or his saints willing him to act for us and who we pray for. And secondly a Transcendental prayer which is as I have explained praying when natures transient response is greatest and that is when the leigh lines of the particular destiny changing paths are close together so that God may help to ensure that the best path is taken.

The theory is that if we can pray more then the world will be better off, which must be in direct response to the increase in transcendental prayer. So if we can train our thought to pray when ever we feel the urge, where ever we are, then surely prayers will be answered more directly. I understand that we can not be talking to our selves all the time. I think that what is needed is simple good thought, which is what most of us do anyway, but when we think of our prayer just to think of the placebo effect will be enough positive direction for the encouragement of active prayer as we know through the science of the Placebo effect that it is effective. This can be known as transcendental prayer.

So from the very small to the very big if thought is effective in this way then what about our evolution? Will a majority of thought lead to an evolution of that thought? Yes think that thought on a large scale may affect response. If this is the case then evolution could be explained as a transient response (Re chapter). Or at least a part of it, but I also believe that Darwin was correct.

Situation Actually

This chapter is all about the moment and how one feels in converse. I can state three extremes of talking to people and I will analyses all three to give you an idea of how it is best to direct your thought.

Firstly one that is concerned only with the present. This can be hard to understand. It is 'direct description' with no hindsight or tangents. It is no more than a list and as such is hard to remember. It has its uses especially in the military. It can feel like trying to remember a deck of cards and is called 'Actual Situation'.

Its counter part is a situation Occasional Scenario which occurs when someone is so concerned with their environment and their super ego that describing a list may be difficult and one may even forget what one is doing as his mind goes off at a tangent so the job will not get done this way either.

The solution is 'Situation Actually' where one must take a balance of what is going on and respond by first catching sight of an occasional scenario and avoid it by switching to Actual Situation for a while.

So the reality is 'Situation Actually' which emphasises the point of physical interaction and the realities of connective material.

Transubstantiation

This is perhaps the most controversial issue to understand without bias as its theology's are at the roots of Christian religion. So I will tread carefully and will try to treat it with the respect that has been placed upon it.

Its definition from the Oxford dictionary is; 'a conversion of whole substance of Eucharistic bread and wine into body and blood respectively of Christ.'

So it is the belief that one thing can become another by devotion. Looking into this idea I have to question my Christian belief, which is, as the Bible tells us, that God was the father of Jesus and not man, because the Catholic Church change the bread and wine into the actual body and blood of Christ by devotion. This leads me to believe that Jesus is the Son of God by devotion, in other words his DNA would say otherwise. I like this idea and yes, Jesus was the Son of God.

However I find that transubstantiation is everywhere from day to day and it comes in the form of transient energy. When for example two people wish to hold hands but have not yet done so, they may be thinking of holding hands and it feels real to both of them. This I call transcendental transubstantiation.

I Won't Do Wrong

Curiously I have been the most involved with transubstantiation whilst smoking in hospital, where the act of drawing breath through the cigarette appeared to be drawing energy from everything around me including other people. This started to worry me, and I felt that it was beginning to annoy others. I found that drawing energy from the atmosphere and from the TV the solution as well as from people's feet. This was also positive as good feet are considered complimentary. All this was enough technique for me to manage my equilibrium (neither a lender nor a borrower be, though it is good to be generous).

The atmosphere in hospital seemed to be a very subconscious and unspoken one as telepathy and non speak seemed to dictate what was going on. As I have explained my understanding of transubstantiation helped me. One thing that really helped through this tense situation was my basic understanding of Thai chi. I was in a fortunate position to have been taught by the best Thai Chi instructor in the country who was a student taught in a direct line from one of the great master. This allowed me to understand any underlying tensions so I could help out where I could and choose the best laid path. It also helped me to find who my friends were and who would help me to do the right thing.

I will explain that 'doing the right thing' is a fulltime job making success of ones transcendentalism, ones Transubstantiation, ones non speak and manner, politeness etc. For if you make a real conscious effort on every little success you can start to build with bricks and also clear a path ahead of you. I liken it to building in bricks because I make sure that any successes are properly laid one on top of the other. This method works even if you have to start at the foundations. And by the time you have finished, the house, you will have earned it and you will feel like a better person.

There is an important issue that I should point out and that is the possibility of Mistransubstantiation which is basically an incorrect manifestation of transubstantiation. This is an awkward thing, but is very preventable. As with most things God will help. It is one of the worst things to experience in the field of psychology as it is Human error and therefore a weakness. It is why I worried whilst smoking in Hospital and why my knowledge in Thai Chi was priceless at that time. This is a good example of Mistransubstantiation which is basically a form of transient error but one that is tangible to the physical.

The worst form of Mistransubstansiation has to be in the form of Voodoo where different animal parts are consumed for their magical properties. Where the rarer the animal the more potent the Voodoo belief is. This sort of practice is what I call a non prayer, where one is fooling, or trying to fool, transience into action. Obviously the evil committed in denying these wonderful creatures their right to live far out weighs any medical Voodoo success. I may state that a non prayer is not a free prayer even if it makes a difference, that difference will be lost somewhere else along the way in this case it is the loss of a great animal and all the good that it could have done. This is Mistransubstantiation at its worst.

Transient Response And Transient Timing

These two theories lie very close together, and can be explained best by writing about them in the same context as I learnt of them my self.

Transient Response

This is a theory that some other intellect can respond to one's thought. This can be best explained by naming it as 'transient response' where an individual's mental space or thought can be responded to. It can be as simple as a packet of crisps falling without anything touching it, and at a very precise moment. This is something that happened to me twice in the same shop at different times and possibly even the same packet of crisps. Though I don't think that is too relevant. The interesting thing is that it occurred both times at the same moment of purchase. The essence of this theory is that the transient response could happen through any medium like the TV creaking, an apple falling from a tree. What this basically means is that we can communicate with God or at least receive guidance from the Holy Spirit and / or the Ultra World. This I call
'Transient Response.'

Transient Timing

This theory states that an action or thought coincides with alarming and exact accuracy with time and act. Again I will use a scenario that relates directly to this point.

Whilst at my lowest point that I had ever found I stayed up all night deciding what I could do to escape my neurosis. I had set the alarm for work the next day. Now all night is a long time. I was in a very bad way. Anyway I decided to sleep at last, as I fell onto my bed at the exact time the alarm went off. Now it was at exactly the same time. The power of this instant unplanned occurrence filled me with adrenalin and shock. This is transient timing, and it can be mapped out over the decades as works of God. The example that I am thinking of is the parting of the Red Sea allowing the Israelites to cross. Suggestion has been made that a tsunami was the cause of this retreat. But it was God that told them to get a move on. This also is Transient timing. And surely the most luminous evidence in the existence of God and his transient plan.

Photographic Memory's and Visions

My theory on the uses of a photographic memory are complex yet strangely attainable and productive. Basically when one wishes for the transient path to improve one may use this, as a second vision, to encourage order and to create more harmonious patterns. A simple thought of calm may be attained by visualising a soul mate, friend or even the gentle lapping of the sea on an empty beach or what ever is the most appropriate thought to help with the 'actual situation'.

It is the art of seeing two things at once. Seeing with the eyes and seeing with the mind. These two methods use different parts of the brain hence they can both run at the same time.

By doing this two things happen: firstly you will be calmed by your favourite vision and secondly everything around you may make more sense to others as well as to yourself.

The trick is not to get lost in your vision but use it to aid converse. You after all must be able to recall what is going on, otherwise you may loose track of your situation. This I call 'occasional scenario'.

Of course I have not studied neurology but my general understanding of the brain leads me to believe this to be likely

Can you invent a vision or does it have to be something that you have already seen? If we take example from the dream where visually you have not seen things before. We can assume that the answer is yes you can invent a vision.

What is the difference between a vision and a photographic memory? A vision is something that is constructed with imagination and is a product of the mind whilst a photographic memory is your mind recalling events visually and accurately. I believe that everyone has to some extent a photographic memory but in varying degrees.

Seeing God

One thing that I have talked about to some extent in my book is hallucination. With the knowledge that I have now I will promote the idea of seeing God. For much of civilisation we have accepted that we can hear God through his Holy Spirit but to see him has not been widely acknowledged.

Essentially hallucination is something usually visual and holographic and which disappears when looked at directly. Seeing God however is seeing a physical pattern that will become stronger the more you look. But, this is the tricky bit, you can hallucinate of the vision of seeing God making the image more vivid. And if you are looking for grace and holiness the figuration will be tainted good where if you are thinking suspicion or vengeance the figurative will morph toward bad. It is if you like guidance from God to keep your mind straight. God gave us freedom of thought and for us to be able to use this gift correctly he will reward us visually for thinking good.

However there is pure hallucination, pure folly, like seeing gnomes and pixies and lepricorns in the bushes on a walk back from the pub at night, maybe this is a side effect of our gift of seeing God or may be it is the joy of being free but more likely it is our ability to see patterns and solve puzzles. So if you can't see clearly then your brain will start to make the most of what it can see and make up the rest. Our brains are well capable of seeing patterns that allow us to notice the difference in objects and ideas and so this hallucination is simply your brain trying to understand what it can not quite see.

The 'Seeing God' epiphany came to me in two stages. Firstly I heard it referenced on TV which intrigued me. Secondly the idea was confirmed and the reality of seeing God came to fruition in my mind when I noticed my initials in the front hedge of my home. HAJ was clearly legible and remained so for three or four weeks. As though it was something that God wished me to notice and keep on noticing until I had realised the obvious link with seeing God. I was also looking for a hot hatch and sure enough in the hedge there were the initials XR3i, a classic old ford escort. Well I looked for one but never found one to buy. Some of you may say that I should not have stopped looking and that I ought to buy one. This is my point where I say drink in tea spoons not pints. For I haven't the space, time or money at the moment but in the future who knows?

This phenomenon has its relevance with life in general, the idea of positive thought encourages life to be better. Like hearing the birds non speak you will be supported, by the birds, if you direct good thoughts whilst listening. I believe this whole arena is here to encourage us to think straight and by thus doing allowing for God's prophecy to develop.

※ *Book 4*

Superstitions

Number Plates and Evolution

I had noticed for quite some time that the relevance of numbers and letters on 'the passing car's number plates' seemed to be associated with my thoughts and this representation came very spontaneously. That is not to say that I sought to check every number plate, just the ones I noticed, when instinct told me to look. There have been, on a rare occasion, times where the transient message has shocked me and it is these moments which inspired me to link by theory the thought of 'natural coincidence' (which is what my number plate observation was hinting at.) into Darwin's theory of evolution. Could it be so that just occasionally something out of the blue happens, out of transience, that could hold the power to change things that otherwise might not have changed. A place where different Leigh lines are close together so that the transient energy between them is at its weakest and they are therefore most able to cross or join each other to produce a new Leigh line of their own. This is my number plate theory.

My thought was then provoked whilst watching a documentary on forest ants. They are blind yet they know instinctively what job they are required to perform (and this is on a huge scale). I deduced that they find it obvious and therefore the transience of the group must be enormous (or the jobs very limited). So if we think that every car be representative of an ant, and we are sure that there is rarely an occasion that we be misled, then we must be obliged to act our own lives around what appears to us to be true or transient. The number plate theory states that this may be done in necessity to find the transient path that one finds very rarely which will illuminate itself for its intrinsic Leigh line progression. If one does not conduct ones self transiently these opportunities may go unnoticed and therefore one is less likely to progress. I suggest that ants have proved that we need only do what appears to be the right thing almost as though our destiny is already planned out. Though planned out it may be but there are places where Leigh lines are close together 'a place where there is little transient resistance in possible life direction', In other words key moments may map out your world and transience will keep your world together. So it is up to us to determine whether we accept or decline the chance of change. Natural selection states that we will take the best laid path but there is an element of chance and it is this chance that adds spice to life.

So if we are wishing to find the best laid path then like the ants we will. And in this theory we will rely on chance for us to personally evolve our lives. The question is what ground does this lay on in the evolution of man? It appears to be neither natural selection nor intelligent design but a mixture of both. It is close to natural selection as one is consciously choosing the best path, but it is also like intelligent design because it relies on the idea of Leigh lines divinely coinciding (the number plate theory).

The concept of intelligent design employs the idea that there is a higher force working with us to evolve. It suggests that God has the evolutionary controls and it is he who will evolve us. We know of the Collective Unconscious and we know that God is likely to harbour its workings (because we know of the Holy Spirit). And therefore it makes sense to expect Gods constant involvement with us to effect our

I Won't Do Wrong

evolution because he is kind and gracious and will therefore help us when and where he deems appropriate.

Also intelligent design opens up a window of potential, allowing us to help our selves to evolve. We know that the conscious mind can affect the physical, as the placebo effect has demonstrated. We also know that it is sincere thought and therefore prayer that can change physical things. So we must therefore expect a Collective Conscious to affect physical life and therefore evolution.

Ultimately evolution is about progressive change and our analysis of this evolutionary change is our belief (collective conscious) and our scientific knowledge.

I have previously stated that prayer works, because of the placebo effect, and so a collective conscious may therefore be a theory of evolution. The idea is that evolution can come from the collective conscious over many hundreds or thousands of years. Evolving within transience allowing us to slowly evolve and adapt to our surroundings.

So there are the two main theories of evolution. Darwin's theory of the Survival of the Fittest and Intelligent Design, where Intelligent Design operates from two sources; the collective unconscious (harboured by God) and the collective conscious harboured by us.

Natural selection relies on the survival of the fittest. The question is does that include chance? Can the chance meeting of two different gene pools, as in the number plate theory, be an attribute of the survival of the fittest and therefore Darwinian logic? I would suppose so but only marginally and I should say that this, my number plate theory, would be included in his work but that it is not the most effective ingredient.

And so does that disprove Intelligent Design? I would suppose not. Not if prayer works as the placebo effect does.

The number plate theory is much less of a worker, than Natural Selection or Intelligent Design, in the process of evolution. But it does have a role to play and that role is to encourage us to realise where opportunities exist. So it is more of a social role encouraging the 'Mere Cat' to search for his own girl and set up a new family. Which is not strictly evolutionary. So we are left with intelligent design and natural selection but which one is the strongest ingredient? I do believe that they both are the key ingredients of evolution but over what time scale and to what effect I don't know?

We know that evolution occurs and that species can take on different characteristics via separation in response to change in their surroundings, and that this can be done quite quickly (i.e. thousands of years). And we know that it will be the ones who best fit their environment and are most capable of surviving that will breed the most. And that is natural selection in a nut shell. So what role does intelligent design have?

This will take some working out.

'Morphic Resonance' is not my term but it explains what I think is important in Intelligent Design. I will give you an example of 'Morphic Resonance' using the example that first drew me towards its possibility; 'When I was younger I remember the birds suddenly started to drink milk from our bottles outside the door where at the same time it was occurring all over the country in Scotland and Wales. Now they all seemed to start at the same time, which to me sounds like Morphic Resonance. Where an idea or belief can travel faster than a letter or plane or anything physical. I know it is a bit of a chancy example but it is neat and tidy and stresses the energy that it is using which has to be the from Spirit World and the fourth dimension. Where the source within the fourth dimension could be from unconscious or conscious encouragement.

I have explained Transient Response and 'Morphic Resonance' could be another example of it, which might explain Adam in the garden of Eden. Of course there was the first Adam but with Morphic Resonance the possibility is that there were many Adams all over Africa at roughly the same time. We know that Humans existed in Africa for about seventy five thousand years before the sea dropped one hundred metres. This allowed small groups to trek through once impassable water crossings to start to populate the world. The clarity of evolution is of course that we are all descendent from the same ape which doesn't exist any more because it has turned into us.

We also know that Humans have lived for about seventy five thousand years outside of Africa. And yet we all have different characteristics. This is undeniably due to new environment and our ability to reflect our surroundings to ensure that we are best able to hunt and live. There is theory that our ancestors, who lived during the ice age suffered from rickets, a gross bone deformation caused by a lack of Vitamin D which is synthesised in the skin in the presence of sun light. And so naturally those in areas of minimal sunlight have lightened the pigment of the skin in order to maximise the minimal sunlight that was around. In physics we learn that dark surfaces absorb light, heating in the process, and so dark skin absorbs likewise, and similarly light skin reflects and so creating more energy at the surface. It is a bit like a karate chop if it breaks the board then it hurts less than if the board does not break.

Therefore the lighter the skin the more efficient it will be at creating Vitimin D.

I really like the idea of Morphic resonance and the more I look into it the more evidence I find to support it. The things that tie this theory together are the workings of God and the workings of the Spirits, where Transtelepathy, (which is a trait of nature), is a form of communication that can travel globally. I call this Morphic resonance.

Is it possible for language to develop with the help of the Spirit World and therefore allow for common ground among neighbouring tribes? Possibly I would say. Language is something that we have thrived on and has been one of our most important evolutionary processes, and with the idea that Morphic Resonance could have escalated its progress which gave rise to and hastened the arrival of the modern man.

Moving on a few thousand years;

Is it possible that Transtelepathical voices that we know today were the voices that tribes could hear and who praised them as the voices of their ancestors? To tell you the truth I don't know because on a personal level I only deal with the Spirit World and the way I choose to live does not include the voices of the deceased. But I would say that this is most likely.

Ultimately it is God who is present to allow life to exist and I believe that it is possible that he works closely with the spirits of our collective unconscious and our collective conscious as pools of information (rather like a library), so that he can direct transience, by understanding the shear mass of minds working for different goals (Intelligent design). However we know that God is present and so there must be a part of him (his Holy Spirit) that can home in on individual prayer. The point of differentiation between the two extremes of our interaction with God is to recognise his intellectual transience and to understand that God has many ways; Firstly the God that sits on high blessing as he sees fit and; Secondly his presence in the holy spirit which can converse with an infinite number of people without falter. I believe that because God is said to have mirrored our minds to reflect his own, he has allowed through the existence of a collective conscious a chance to have a real impact on our evolution. This would go unnoticed as it is a notion (like the placebo) that can be very slow to affect. So I believe that Natural Selection and Intelligent Design cooperate in the field of evolution, to such an extent even that they may be the only factors involved but most likely they are the only factors that carry any weight and that they do so equally.

In Addition To Previous Text

With hindsight this intrinsic recognition of 'number plates' may simply show that my mind was working in a very cognitive yet unrelenting state of alert. However I have done this, 'plan air' so to speak, to my satisfaction.

This is a real arena in the psychic world, but for me the fruits of blindly following transience around are not worth while because God has mirrored our minds on his. So to follow God's transience around in this manner would be to ignore your own transience, which if ignored will be taken only as folly in your own mind and that will cause confusion. To have done this successfully (i.e. to prove that there is an arena there), either shows a strong connection with Transience or that I was underestimating my cognitive skills and determined to make sense of chaos which was using my intuition in this manner for self recognition, which at the time I craved. But it felt a lot more real than folly and coincidence at the time. I was finding life tough and needed to boost my confidence which involved certain philosophical success to show my own mind to be correct, which mostly I thought it was. Anyhow I like this theory. Of course this was the reason for the chapter and was an inspiration that encouraged me to continue, which seemed very natural at the time. I do not now however read plates as religiously as before. It was a stage in my life and as far as I was concerned it proved itself correct within my own science. It helped me at the time. Hence this chapter, but now I must leave it alone for it can offer me now nothing that I need.

The Manner of Object Significance Or Transubstantiation of Matter

Crystal balls, Taro cards and tea leaves? Is there a tangible link to the wider world for this type of fortune telling? Can buying from gypsies bring good luck? Could a clairvoyant perform mystical tasks? Yes, it is possible to predict and to examine someone for traits of the subconscious, but this is a product of telepathy as well a transient examination. There is a place in your transcendental mind that can be visible especially to those on the same wavelength (retranscendental) but unable to change the things that the transcendental can and so these folk make for good analysers of transient situations. It must be said that this is a very intrinsic trait (retranscendental) and very rare, but you may very well meet someone who confirms this theory for you.

As for taro cards, well I have a story about card prediction. It happened whilst I was in hospital, when I was at my most transient.

It was a clear decision. Should I pursue a friendship or not? At least the signs were pointing toward yes, but my mind was not so sure. I had a deck of cards and thought that I should pick a card to see if I was on the right line. So I did and I picked a King of Hearts. Still not enough. So I picked again and to my surprise it was a Queen of Diamonds, I picked again and drew the Jack of Diamonds or Clubs (I can't remember exactly). And then someone else came whom I thought was also liking this person, so I picked for me and got the two of clubs and picked for him and it was the two of diamonds I walked away. But this situation was not important. We were all simply doing our best and learning what we could in a very boring environment. The importance is this surreally accurate card prediction, the magic of which has stayed with me, and as if God has thrown down the gauntlet he has left me wondering about all sorts of transient offerings and situations. Hope is the most valuable thing that he has given me as well as faith.

The evidence of magic here is plain, but whose magic was it? There are a few possibilities; Firstly was it my magic as a highly transcendental student, Secondly was it the form the 'Ultra World' and the Collective Unconscious or the physical world of the Collective Conscious. Or Thirdly was it the Holy Sprit or Fourth was it the word of God our Lord on High?

Well I can rule out the collective conscious as there were no other minds that could have been bought into play. So was it the collective unconscious? This seems like a good contender. As does the thought of it being in part, my own mind's magic as a leading transcendental. Now these two, personal transience and the collective unconscious/conscious, run on the same tape in other words they can help each other with the same weight. They are in the same ball park playing the same game.

The Holy Spirit is our personal God and he/she knows everything about us like a parent does his children, this does not mean that he can not be blind to some action his son has taken but that he will understand once the confessions are heard. The Holy Spirit is our closest link to God. Except that I believe we can and do talk to God and I think that it must be a situation similar to that of voice hearing where

I Won't Do Wrong

he may similarly slip into the ultra world and conduct in the same way as we do out of our conscious minds Gods presence in this state is called the Holy Spirit, though I am sure that when transience spontaneously invites him into the physical he will as we do pick up the chalice and do his best. He visits whenever transience directs much like super man the Holy Spirit is there for you always. This theory is a contender. I think that the Holy Spirit is a likely source but not that it was a direct call from our Lord God, more like the advice of one of his workers who will have more time for trivial matters.

So was this guidance from above? Yes and No, in my view we interact with God whose truth comes in the form of 'Transient Response and Transient Timing' where transient response gives us a direct line to God. And Transient Timing gives us the indelible proof of his interaction with the world. which may be acting on the sincerity of mind. I believe it is sincerity that conducts such magic. (Which is why Voodoo appears to work which bothers me because this could be averted by praying through the spirit of an animal, and not by the butchering of it: that would be a genuine prayer because when God will see grace he will offer effective support.(Re ch. Transubstantiation). We must remember that the placebo effect is real but relatively weak, so if medication is offered then it should be accepted, because you will more likely be helped with the magic of modern day

Some examples of transubstantiation come with personal experience whilst finding Excalibur and the Philosophers stone, (on separate occasions). The first that got me wondering was the reliance of cards whilst deciding whether or not to pursue a friendship to help out or not I picked on a deck of cards and got some amazing results. I picked the queen of diamonds, the King of Hearts followed by the jack of diamonds and to decide whether or not I should help or not a two of clubs for me and a two of diamonds for my man next to me. That was it. It was not life or death so I walked away.

Whilst attending an A' Level art class I noticed a drawing. It was of a man carrying his girl. And her dress had blown up in the wind but they were oblivious or non caring about it. The fact that you could see the colour of her knickers and that they were both too preoccupied to notice led to a realisation that one must remember that there is more in the world than just you and I.

Many years later I was walking a beach at sun rise and I came upon a stone with the very same inscription as the drawing on one side and a representation of a dragon fly or someone with a shield or someone carrying the girl as before but with knickers free from the prying eye.

This stone felt more like a coin and it was perfect except for a knobble of something. Its intrinsic design seemed too coincidental for me not to acknowledge a connection, and I have kept this stone for I was sure it harboured power, I may pick it up again some time but for the moment I will leave it.

Another example is my finding Excalibur as talked about in 'Gone Missing' and how I found it in the form of a simple wooden stick tapered and perfectly finished with four stems near the handle for hand protection. This was Excalibur but I was so unsure of myself that I returned it to the supernatural in order for it to be found again in whatever form and to whomever's sincerity deserves it. Yes it gave me strength and yes I was not sure how to control its transient power, but I found it if only for a while.

This leads me to the point of the placebo and prayer. Sometimes we need a little help to maintain our lives which is where prayer and placebo work in offering hope and hope is what promotes transient action.

If one feels the need for redemption, this mainly concerns those who may not have had faith and those who have just acquired it. It is possible to metaphorically 'carry the cross' and if this is done the world will redeem. Yes he did this for us.

On a lighter note, I will explain my position on the existence of the Holy Grail. My sixpence worth is simpler and yet more accessible than other theories. I suggest that if you are looking for it then you will surely find it but that you will not realise until you stop looking.

In essence the idealism of the grail to me is the fact that I believe people already have it. Psycho-Synthetically it fits within the torso it should be shaped as a vessel and it unites the organs of the body with the spirit of God or for Jesus name. It will keep you strong and will help keep you healthy, it is strong but needs looking after. It may be a measure of ones constitution if you regard it as a vessel, in that you may feel when it is low and you may feel when it is being topped up.

The grail is a gift to the wise where opinion and choice are concluded with retrospect and compassion assuring that the best is done, and it is a wonderful thing to own.

It is possible to lose the grail but it is always there to be found again.

Quality of Food

Food is there for us to feed on and enjoy as befits the individual. I have been through some tough times and food nearly always entered into my psychic welfare. How it was cooked to the precision of ingredients, the time of eating and the company that I was eating with.

Herbs were my first investigation. This began with Marjoram and Basil which were among my top herbs. This is putting an over emphasis on their properties as herbs but at the time I considered, clear as day, the obvious and correct use of them was for the magic they contained, and surely for specific occasions?(re non prayer)

The above was a bit too psychosomatic, (ie putting too much stress on superstition) because as any good chief will tell you different herbs do best with different dishes, but it wont change the world if he spills in the wrong herb.

More interestingly I can reveal that whilst eating mainly fruit my skin, most noticeably my fingers became dry and shiny and even cracked without bleeding for apparently only supernatural reasons and refused to heal.

This occurred after being warned that there is a scenario where glass can be the medium for transient magic. The same had happened to a friend of mine. He said don't touch broken glass. Well I did try to clear some up. I bent down touched the glass very lightly and saw a plasmatic pulse of light. I looked at my thumb and there was a small gash, it did not bleed but it was deep.

I paid no attention to this for a while until the index finger (next to the affected thumb) got the same stigma. They would not go away. And that for me was a sign from God saying open your door and you will see all of the magic in the world. But it was probably the effect of the simple diet of fruit and very little else.

Another stigma that I noticed was that I had a sparkly moustache. I shaved daily but there was something that made my upper lip sparkle. I put this down to the fruit but it may have been transient effect adorning me with a sparkle.

Artists colour

As an artist and a philosopher I feel that it would not be right to leave this subject without explaining the theory of colour narrative. I will therefore run through the colours and shades of the spectrum in order for their transient meaning to be exposed.

Firstly I shall analyse purple:

Purple can be used as a form of righteousness. It is a royal colour and suits the matriarch image well, and expresses the vital role of the wise matriarchal figure. It is a divine colour sometimes offering religious connotation.

Red is also a royal colour. It is passionate and represents the courage of protecting Purple (say). Red has many shades and likewise many transient meanings. Crimson and Scarlet are of course very different. Where scarlet is much brighter which expresses liveliness and daring, where Crimson is a richer and darker colour expressing comfort and contentment. Pink is a girls colour as blue is a boys it can easily represent kindness of nature as it links itself with a contentment with every thing Human.

Blue is a cool colour. It is calm and suggests a notion of being understanding and laid back. The hues of blue are also varied. There is turquoise which suggests something slightly unique, Oxford blue something intelligent and Prussian blue which is stormy like a role of thunder. But we have the lighter blues including Cambridge blue which gives us the intellect of the calmer blues.

I Won't Do Wrong

Yellow is a difficult colour to analyse as its various shades can represent different things. From the baby light yellow with the aptitude of just existing which is as good as gold, to the associated cowardice of custard yellow which stems from the fact that it is the brightest of the colours that are not all around us in the natural world. In other words it sticks out like a sore thumb, and in the modern day it says, hey I'm doing ok. But it has been used to tarnish things that were weak and lack lustre. It can be a colour that celebrates individuality and a sense of being proud. It is also sometimes regarded as mellow yellow and that is to be cherished. So it is a colour with an ultra ego as it represents both right and left wing social stand points.

Green as with blue has calming shades because nearly everything around us that grows is green. Other shades of it though can be envious (this is a stronger high hue green, arguably the richest and the brightest green pigment) but it also has the pea green of homeliness with the essence of rolling hills and dogs running through meadows.

Orange is a colour that is saying I am over here and could express something that has not been given enough acknowledgement. It is crying out for attention. It is the rarest of natural colours and something that will always stand out. But it could also be a warning or acknowledgment of toxicity.

Brown is a rich earthly colour and can be as sweet as chocolate or as fundamental as barren land (lighter shade) or as fertile as the ploughed field (generally darker) containing the moist richness needed for the next crop. Brown is close to gold as red is close to green and blue to orange. The pigments of the Human skin are shades of brown and the darker the brown the hotter the environment (generally) and we reach out for brown as the indigenous people of these hotter places are brown and this is something that we add to the colour chart through Human emotion and not simply aesthetic balance. We are concerned with plight of the poor in other places and so we recognise charitable thoughts as well as aesthetic ones.

Black and White go together as they are opposites and fundamentally say 'This is this and that is that' clear as day. They are opposites as sunlight soaks into black and reflects off white, so in hot places houses are painted white.

The H.A.J. Number Theorem And Three Number Critique Tag

I had been considering a theory of numerical significance for some time. Challenging the coincidence of numerical patterns that suggest something more than the mathematical.

The first draft of this 'My Number Theorem' which I conducted with the aid of the Egypt Pyramids, as a base for analysis of permutations and relationships between the different sized entities. It introduced the idea of 'Fractorial Analysis' which in easy terms means—that a number can be explained (i.e. its personality) by the application of a simple equation. This method has its foundations of truth as a result of looking at the pyramids. This I will explain shortly. The basic theory is that if the foundations are correct then everything worked out from them must also be inherently correct so long as it follows the same logic.

It is only a theory. There is however enough evidence to connect the personality links as tangible. I have backed my theory up with a mathematical equation that can be applied to a number in order to verify its authenticity as an abstract entity whose personality can therefore be reified. I have also introduced an analytical 'Three Number Critique Tag' that we can all calculate in order to portray our personality in numbers.

I will explain by giving you a small insight into the origins of my study:

If number 1 is alone it is direct and explicitly itself; a metaphor could be that it is direct current or one dimension. And number 2 being double and therefore has the ability for alternating current and has two dimensions. So 2 has numbers that can learn from one an other and therefore 2 has the ability to alter things (as two minds would), or two men may fight in the boxing ring or ultimately two people loving each other, who can change things by reproducing, And so number 2 has the ability to change things. It is a controlling number and the number that dictates change for the majority (e.g. war and politics). It has the power to reproduce or to cull. Number 2 represents an intrinsic position of creating order out of chaos.

Now I suggest that the number 3 is the 'magic' number and is representative of the third dimension, it is the product of parenting and as such can be considered as a containing in its make up two large pyramids (parents) and one small pyramid (or Child and so without three there would be nothing.

Simply put the pyramids made me think of numbers initially with the idea that three is best explained as two large entities and a third smaller one. And it is this revelation that inspired me to think of my number theorem because it referenced three as being a continuum of 1 and 2 and that for my science smaller. And so by knowing that 1, 2 and 3 are the bed rocks of our physical world we can start to explore what else is there to find. This is how I began to analyse numerical personalities, which already existed to some as superstition. I am only firming up the ground by adding proof that this superstition lies closer to the surface than pure speculation.

I Won't Do Wrong

This is where I lay the foundations of my analysis.

The equations below can be applied to all numbers below 100, where X is the number to be analysed (it must be remembered that this equation uses only whole numbers because three is made up of Two large One small). It is a progression method so to try a number over 40 may prove diluting which is where the three tag critique is applicable.

X/2 = A + B

2A/3 (rounded up)+ 2B/3(rounded up) = Majors

Please note that the equation deals only with whole numbers this is due to the minor always being the last of the three count. It is however not necessary to calculate the minors via a complex equation as they can be deduced from the number of majors because the total number of majors and minors must equal the value of X. I must also state that where majors are fractions they must be rounded up. This can be done after the two derivatives have been calculated and added together. So to help understanding I have completed the arithmetic relating to the numbers 1 to 15 using the explained equation.

X=1
    1/2 : 0.5 @ 0.5

Majors 2/3 x 0.5 @ 2/3 x 0.5 - 2/6 + 2/6 = 4/6 = 1

Answer 1 major.

X = 2

2/2 : 1 @ 1

Majors $2/3 \times 1$ @ $2/3 \times 1 \sim 2/3 + 2/3 = 4/3 \Rightarrow 2$

Answer 2 major (rounded up)

X = 3

3/2 : 1 @ 2

$2/3 \times 1$ @ $2/3 \times 2 \sim 2/3 + 4/3 = 6/3 = 2$

So answer 2 major @ 1 minor

X = 4

4/2 : 2 @ 2

$2/3 \times 2$ @ $2/3 \times 2 \sim 4/3 + 4/3 =$ (rounded up) $= 2 + 2 = 4$

Answer Majors = 4

X = 5

5/2 : 2 @ 3

Majors ; $2/3 \times 2$ @ $2/3 \times 3 \sim 4/3 + 6/3 =$ (rounded up) $2 + 2 = 4$

Answer Majors 4 @ Minors = 1

X = 6

6/2 : 3 @ 3

I Won't Do Wrong

Majors ; 2/3 x 3 @ 2/3 x 3 - 6/3 + 6/3 => 4

Answer Majors 4 @ Minors 2

X = 7

    7/2 : 3 @ 4

Majors ; 2/3 x 3 @ 2/3 x 4 - 6/3 + 8/3 => (rounded up) => 2 and 3 => 5

Answer 5 Majors @ 2 Minor

X = 8

    8/2 : 4 @ 4

Majors ; 2/3x4@2/3x4-8/3+8/3=>roundedup=>3+3

Rounded up => 6

Answer Majors 6 @ Minors 2

With the method understood I shall give the answers up to number 15.

X = 9

    Majors 7 @ Minors 2

X = 10

>Majors 8 @ Minors 2

X = 11

>Majors 8 @ Minors 3

X = 12

>Majors 8 @ Minors 4

X = 13

>Majors 9 @ Minors 4

X = 14

>Major 10 @ Minor 4

X = 15

>Major 11 @ Minor 4

Now that we have an insight as to where numbers are in the DNA as it were, we must begin to express the relevance of this mathematical situation. And as with the equation I will get all the answers from numbers 1, 2 and 3 which I have suggested are the correct building blocks for numerical significance.

This can be done by explaining the second part of my theorem. 'The Three Number Tag Critique' which has been

I Won't Do Wrong

calculated from a clear understanding of the numbers 1,2 and 3.

So what is the three number tag critique? Well it is three columns where the first column is for sacrifice and helping from the heart; the second column a fighting or controlling number and the third column is one that stands for wisdom and hindsight.

It is my understanding that each column at its most extreme is as follows;

Number 1 ; represents a quantum of holiness and sacrifice and unselfishness.

Number 2 ; should quantify a leader of men and the manner in which that control is personified. This extreme is the opposite to number one in order to reflect the opposites of an AC current and therefore the strongest to change a notion.

Number 3 ; is a number that most appropriates our spontaneous existence with the knowledge and hindsight and with the awareness of both 1 and 2, it is therefore a number that requires ones wisdom.

The chronology of these entities is important (i.e. Good first, bad second and learned third). This is a natural assemblage as one will fight for what is good and reason over what is bad. Creating wisdom with the use of hindsight and experience.

I will put some faces to these numbers;

Number 1 could represent Jesus
Number 2 could represent Hitler

Number 3 could represent a utopian existence with wisdom, or a personal state of mind. And to put a person to the equation ; Nelson Mandela

I am not suggesting that people can now never reach these extremes, but more that the limits of these extremes have already occurred and therefore the boundaries for this model have been mapped out. The question now is how can this edge us closer toward a utopian existence? Well if there should be a mass request for transient peace and living, which can only be the product of passive existence. Then with an eye to help the world go by and an acknowledgement that we are all here on earth at the same time in a history of billions of years, coexistence must be paramount to success, where we may say in our after lives on meeting another spirit 'Oh I was on Earth then too, where were you?' Only then may we be close enough to our selves to allow a speedy progression toward God's prophecy and what it is he has prepared for us.

It shows at what lengths people will go to in pursuit of desire and because of these examples it is possible to look at yourself and calculate your own three letter tag critique. This may change with time so there are no certainties just a chance to self analyse ones self for no other gratification than personal interest.

So theologically it is possible to work out every number and their respective character if we agree that the numbers 1,2 and 3 are suitably analysed and understood for this particular model.

All numbers have an intrinsic relevance for someone, whether it be birthdays or any number obtained during

I Won't Do Wrong

you life's worth of important observations / events etc. This expression of numerical emotion can be so perfectly compelling as to be completing, in other words there is a three number tag for every one and that it may fit like a glove and it can give one a more rock steady opinion of oneself, by giving some sort of order in the chaos. It may free ones inner person a little as it fascinates by giving a surprisingly simple yet accurate personality analysis.

What do the lower numbers offer as intrinsic meaning? I will start by offering you a low down of the numerical characteristics I am analysing.

We know about 1,2 and 3 so I will start with 4.

Four is a wild number that will spark on tangents but while unpredictable it can be a very good explorer.

> Five is a self help number
> Six is the most efficient number
> Seven is for reflection and contemplation
> Eight is for truth finding
> Nine is for loudness
> Ten is for a complete arena
> Eleven is a wild card
> Twelve is for reason and justice
> Thirteen is for luck
> Fourteen is a wild number tamed and good for analysis
> Fifteen is for strength and honour

Explaining the reason behind the common assimilation that the Devils number is said to be 666.

Six as we know is the most efficient number, God made the world in six days but on the seventh he rested. It is easy to analyse therefore that man needs a day of rest and that without which there would be no time for reflection and the good that comes from that. How else can you see your mistakes and thence rectify any wrongs that six may have unearthed.

Number six therefore has the danger of not even being aware of error. So wrong must therefore be a working hazard or a fixed cost. We know that six has a certain vulnerability and it is because of this the number six is used three times in reference of wrong doings.

It is not the case that number six is a bad number because it is not it has its strengths and weaknesses like any other.

For a six to do wrong could be unpredicted and even unnoticed but for a seven to do wrong, well that is much worse as it allows the space for premeditation.

No my theory is not to tell you that some numbers are better than others because that is simply not true. No mine is to describe the personality of that wrong.

For a little more insight into the origins of the building blocks of my theorem I should state that for construction to occur by simulation (allowing the pyramids to take on organic properties such as reproduction (for my model alone)). It would logistically be that each pyramid would comprise three distant pyramids. For the large pyramid should be constructed of two large and one small and for the small pyramids two small and one large there being so due to genetic manifestation. In the real world numbers 1,2 and 3 if we look at dimensions are all the same size however there is space in my theory to suggest that number 3 is smaller as a child (or small pyramid) But for factorial

I Won't Do Wrong

analysis it is only the ratio that matters. The simple magic of the number three helps link my ideas of factorial analysis with its derivatives of two major and one minor.

With the understanding of the term factorial analysis and by using the equation talked of earlier I will show how numbers four to fifteen (as we know the numbers 1,2 and 3) can be expressed in a more than mathematical way. (This is slightly repeated but worth a scan.)

$X = 4$; majors 4 minors 0 ; This is the highest number without minors and its venom is therefore direct and sharp. 4 will remain a number of courage but the accuracy of the venom may be uncalculated.

$X = 5$; majors 4 minors 1 ; This is a self help number with the venom of 4 acting with the loyalty of 1, which is direct and honest.

$X = 6$; majors 4 minors 2 ; The venom of 4 acting with the fighting number 2 gives us six which is the most efficient number because of its factorial composites. It is however vulnerable to oversight. Things may be missed and because it is the most efficient number. It is likely to plough on ahead oblivious to tangents.

$X = 7$; majors 5 minors 2 ; With 5 as a self help number and 2 as the confrontation number, 7 is a number that has positivity and reflection. If wrong is done by this number it may be doubly wrong as one would not wish harm on ones self and five the self help number is inherent in seven and will therefore protect 7's activity. With this inherent hindsight there is therefore the risk of 'calamity' if things of a conscious nature go wrong because number 7 is a number with a self perpetuating sense of guidance which must be over run for wrong to be done.

X = 8; majors 6 minors 2 ; This number is probing its surroundings. It is a truth number with the efficiency of 6 and the confrontation of 2. It is most direct and unforgiving, which is the best way to get to the truth. It is a truth finding number.

X = 9; majors 7 minors 2 ; This is a loudness number. With the self productivity of 7 and the confrontation of 2 make it ideal for the mega phone.

X = 10; majors 8 minors 2 ; This is a number that is very contained with the confidence and enquiry of 8 and the confrontation of 2.

X = 11; majors 8 minors 3 ; With the confidence and enquiry of 8 and the magic that surrounds 3. Number 11 is the wild card a number that can search out patterns of a genuine but spurious nature.

X = 12; majors 8 minors 4 ; With the ability for detecting truth of 8 and the liveliness of 4. Where 4 will be judged by 8 working carefully to sift out the truth of 4's findings. Makes this a good number for jurisdiction.

X = 13; majors 9 minors 4 ; With the loudness of 9 but with the inaccuracy and potency of 4 errors may be possible, but extra interesting results are also expected. It is a luck number good and bad.

X = 14; majors 10 minors 4; With the number 10 anchoring number 4 preventing its intrinsic inaccuracies. (or direction of venom) these two numbers work together to perform accurate analysis and calculation.

X = 15; majors 11 minors 4; with the potential of 11's ability to locate spurious directions given the raw power of

4. This is a number that protects. It is an abrasive number with lots of gusto. It is strong and prepared to take a fall.

I Won't Do Wrong

This method becomes harder to read when the numbers are distant from the original three as it is an accumulative model. I will therefore suggest that the three number critique tag may be used for these higher numbers.

That is by using the three column method;

For example;

Number 127 can be understood as a
>Number 1 in column 1
>Number 2 in column 2
>Number 7 in column 3

This can be read as some one who devotes the right quantity of humble admiration in column 1. And the right quantity of fight in column 2. Though with a 7 in column 3 this person, with an apt ability for doing well, is seen with the retrospect of 7 and so here is someone with confidence, who will conduct themselves honourably and with the self assured strength of correctness.

This is my number theorem, it states links with the significance of numbers in relation to things other than mathematical. I have written it to quell my intrigue and curiosity. It must be remembered that no number is a predetermining factor for wrong doing. I will simply suggest that different numbers are susceptible to different kinds of wrong. And that destiny has a road for everyone and it is our role to do what we can to make the most of the precious life we lead.

For completion I will put forward the susceptible errors of each of the numbers from 1-15.

1 is likely to be blind to motives outside of a cocoon. It can be purely an act for ones self and for the appreciation of ones self.

2 is likely to be a fighting error like a wild punch up with no real motives.

3 is likely to be a whole hearted simple act of error where the person knows what he/she is doing but cares not because it makes sense (to him/her).

4 is likely to be sporadic and full of venom (a bit wild)

5 is likely to be precious like protecting a certain property or person that is close to his/her's fundaments.

6 is likely to be matter of fact simply 'that needs to be done for this to happen' with no heart rendering notion.

7 is likely to be planned or desperate, one or the other, and has its roots in injustice. This act may weigh heavy on his/her mind.

8 is likely to be planned and a calculated act, possibly for justice or something important.

9 is likely to be loud misconstruing 'actual situation', or over doing a job.

10 is likely to be an exact knowledge of action with cause and consequence worked out to quantify the action, it will be an obvious act, harbouring no delusion.

11 is likely to be out of the blue and may result in something catastrophic done without full appreciation of the consequences

12 is likely to be misunderstanding a scenario but not without lengthy consideration.

13 is likely to be unfair

14 is likely to be well calculated and direct completing a job with all corners covered

I Won't Do Wrong

15 is likely to be a large force to achieve a goal in order to protect something categorically correct and unable to protect itself.

Finally I should state that each of the columns has a trump card column

$$1 - 7$$
$$2 - 6$$
$$3 - 8$$

Here I have used number six for column two where previously I have stated that Hitler may be number two. The truth is that his number could easily have been a seven. It is his pure evil that made his analysis of himself seem good.

One thing that I must state is that no one has more propensity for doing wrong than any one else. It is only the manner of wrong not the quantity of wrong that I am suggesting may fit this model.

Hopefully this theorem will intrigue you.

Green Day

Iris had taken just about as much as she could, she threw the half emptied cup of coffee across the room. Immediately she regretted the mess and was surprised by the quantity and ferocity of her anger. She was living in a flat she didn't like, in a building containing fifteen other flats and twenty five people all of which she sneered at except one. She resented them for their sobriety and their normality but mostly it was their content approach and happiness with the life that they were leading. She often mimicked them for their lack of ambition and drive but if only she could drop the heroin. She was green with envy and her bark and bite could be heard near everywhere she went. Because secretly she wanted to be just like them.

She reached across to the end of the coffee table and picked up her stash of cannabis and rizla and rolled herself a strong joint and started to think.

She had been resident in the flat for close on a year and the walls were becoming too familiar. It was not a tidy flat but when she had first moved she had plans to turn it into her little love nest, her home and somewhere to feel safe in. So although she was tidy by nature her situation had forced her to be complacent until all of a sudden her lovely little place to be cosy in looked only a little better than a squat. She had been to a squat before, on her quest for the drug, and although she seemed helpless at the moment she had better ideas for herself than that

I Won't Do Wrong

There had been a few friends around again. It was not like she didn't want them there, well not until now, she thought. But here they were crashed out in her front room. Over on the table there was a syringe and a charred metal spoon. This was exactly how she had seen the arena of self destruction when she was a child on the telly and that memory, the memory of how she felt, shock, distaste and fear, a lot of fear, consumed her throughout. She pulled herself up from the couch that had been her bed on the previous night, (her own had been taken over by a couple, the man of which she knew.) It was still her bed which peeved her but her head was too thick to bother, she stood and scanned the room.

There was in the corner of the lounge laying on a settee a handbag. It was Charlene's, her only real friend who lived in an upstairs flat. Iris knew that it was Charlene's because everything she owned glowed in her eye's. She offered hope and normality and in her life at the moment she was the only one that could help her and genuinely her only real friend. The money was still there, of which she was undyingly grateful, some of those around her would not have thought twice about taking money that just seemed to be doing nothing. So pleased with her find she went up the stairs and knocked on her door.

The door opened and a frizzy haired tired looking lady answered: "Oh it's you."

"Hand bag." Iris offered the bag to Charlene

"What's it like downstairs?" Asked Charlene

"It's a mess, a lot of them still snoring can we get rid of them?"

"You mean can I help you to get rid! I'll be down in five." Charlene said and closed the door to get ready.

Iris got a little depressed and frightened as she looked around the room and then at her veins on her inner arm, this had gone too far and she knew this had to be a turning point. She could not let heroin take her life the way it always seemed to in the news and as it clearly had to some of those around her.

Wondering around she saw Charlene at the door and just said: "Thank you." They were soon to empty the flat of what she saw as a handful of helpless people.

For the first time she really felt low and wondered what day it was. Thursday; Giro day. If there was one thing that she had to do was to make it to the job centre and convince them that she was still looking for work, which she found easy to do, as she had a qualification that allowed her to look for work in a specific field of employment. But boy she looked rough this morning, surely someone would say something!

Charlene was a real peoples person she would have been a real NHS hero if her upbringing had been more in line. And with the both of them active the flat was soon emptied. "I am kind but we are not a hostel" Iris had to say to one or two that didn't want to move because there was no where to go to. These two of whom both Iris and Charlene felt sorry for were given toast and coffee before uprooted and persuaded through the door.

Iris went by herself to the job centre and was not waiting long befor it was her time in the hot seat:

"Have you made any enquiries . . . uhm . . . Iris?"

"Um . . . yes there was a junior position at an accident compensation company in town." (She had seen this advertised on the boards while waiting to see someone.)

I Won't Do Wrong

"Yes, you have a law degree . . . collected two thousand and three. But you have been out of work for . . . two and a half years now. Why is that?" And without waiting for an answer he carried on: "We have a detox centre that I think you should go to."

The very idea that she had been sust so quickly by someone who she had never met before stunned her and she found it impossible to speak, her breathing went shallow and she felt really self conscious, embarrassed even.

"Yes." She said whilst wondering what the question was and who had answered. It sounded like her. She held her cool and just looked at him.

"Go here at two tomorrow and ask for Lindsy, you will like her. Sign here and here, thankyou . . . bye."

Iris had in her hands the paper that she needed from the job centre and walked unnervingly back to her flat. She needed a fix so she walked past her suppliers and got herself a ten pound bag. With the folded paper in one pocket and the score in her hand her psyche was flipping madly from one option to the other. In her mind there was a battle going on she remembered the mornings emotion that had so impacted on her to throw her coffee across the room, which she retrospectively thought must be a real sign that all is not well because such behaviour was out of character.

This was only a few hours old but she wasn't ready to accept her lot, she just did what she could do and so rational thought began to leave, and with it any thought of the next day leaving alone the future she sat back in her flat emptied her pockets, she made herself a coffee and sat down to read the blurb that she had been given. She was beginning to withdraw and was sweating her eyes twitching toward the score on the table and her cigarettes. She had scored that morning but there were definitely some good cogs moving inside her. Addiction is strange but I suppose logical in that the idea of giving up, pushed her to want to use even more, the fact of finiteness the lack of one thing you like or need the most, plays tricks on the mind and can cause a real hunger for that one thing. Whether it be drink ciggies drugs, gambling or chocolate.

Still she took the hit, but it was different this time, the first few moments when the drug reached her brain, she used to call wonderful, but it wasn't this time. It was relief but only for a few moments until she began to worry about having taken it, she was paranoid. She knew that she didn't want to have taken it, but she had, and now it will take a few hours of paranoia she knew this. But the intensity it provoked she did not foresee. It wasn't simply the wrong headspace required to fit the day, a longing sense of failure washed over the whole of her living. Damn she was disappointed. She needed to be alone, and felt sure that she would freak out if she had to see anyone. So she shut the curtains locked the door and hoped that no one would bother her.

Five hours and twenty cigarettes later she felt more human again. She needed to go to the shops for something for dinner, she needed a good hearty meal. She sure had not done so for a while. She was in a position that didn't feel so familiar, she was craving normality. To step into her ever so capable shoes of yester year, which let her realise the wows and abandonment of her present life. While she was out she needed another hit though she did not want to tread on her new found shoes. All the worries of the paranoid morning had left her. She even had a spring in her step. However as an addict her mind was still hiding the same worries. She was still thinking, when she got to the shop.

There was a choice of microwave meals, the type she often ate, she bought her favourite, chicken tika mussala.

And picked up a loaf of bread and some cigarettes. She was on her way home when she realised that she had not scored, and although it slowed her pace with indecision she was at her front door faster than the urge to change her route home. And that in my book is strike one.

When was her appointment, leafing through the bills mags and other stuff on the table she found the appointment card 'Two O'clock' she immediately looked at her watch a quarter to six. Time to eat and she went to warm the curry and put some toast on. Shame she had no garlic bread she prepared another slice of bread for the toaster.

Ping! umm scrummy she uttered and slicing the toast into heavily buttered soldiers went into the front room cleared a space on the table and began to eat. A bit compulsively but still she was on her own and it was nicer than she had noticed at any time recently.

Before long the plate was finished and she sat back and lit a cigarette and turned on the telly.

Chapter Two

Picking up the remote Iris flicked on the teletext straight to page 120 revealing something about the weather and love stars or something. Damn she thought it's on BBC and typed in 606 for the now and next. She used to hate this because if you miss a number you have to dial 666 to restart and she had been a bit superstitious about that sort of thing. However she decided now that she didn't really care. She wanted to be sure about positive things and not to burden her mind with trivia, and so she read on;

BBC 2

The Blues Brothers 7.45

This attracted her attention. You know one of those films that everyone has seen and has often been the centre of much mimicking etc. One of those films that she just knew she had to see.

Glancing at her watch she read 7.05, as her mind went blank she stood up quickly for these are the times with the most pangs. Coffee she decreed stood up took out her plate and put on the kettle. One tea spoon and hesitated two tea spoons a dash of milk and stirred it anti clockwise one two three tap tap.

I don't know that she was expecting to enjoy the film or not, the fact is, she watched it and was now able to describe

I Won't Do Wrong

any part of it at any time. One thing she had been looking forward to was the car crash said to have been the biggest pile up ever and now she knew why. Fabulous fun she thought. Comic, not realistic, but sure enough it went on longer than the slow train from Glasgow to London. The humour was spot on and the jamming phenomenal, really quite inspiring, yes she really did like it.

There was a knock at the door. Iris was feeling human again and hoped it was her friend from upstairs Charlene, and sure enough it was. A warmth entered the room a sort of bubbly exuberance altered the atmosphere and every thing seemed a bit better.

Charlene sat down and took out a small bag of marijuana. Now the funny thing about marijuana is that it seems such a sociable thing to do. But it is isolating and responsible for many a psychosis. Like heroin, Iris thought, being friends with users lets ones mind be content with a sort of justification and empathy, but outside of this cocoon lays a world that feels somewhat alien to the user, and the longer it continues the stronger these symptoms exist and the further from society you will feel.

However she needed to talk and Charlene was not a heroin user but Iris had seen this before (in herself) it would not be long before temptation, through intrigue and curiosity, would lead to experimentation and use. So she rolled a joint for the purpose of communing as true as she could. The best ideas are after a joint. Well that is not true but at least in this instant to be on the thing that you want to give up could sort of somehow empower the idea or is that just what it felt like at the time?

"I'm going to stop." She said.

Charlene knew what she meant. "Good." She said, and that was all. She was staring at a painting on the wall a painting that had grabbed he attention on previous occasions. It was very brightly coloured and suggestive of the figurative.

"How?" She asked after a long pause.

"I was given this by the job centre." She passed the appointment time to Charlene.

"You are brave and right, I was going to ask for a little smoke of it tonight just you know to see what it was like. But with you saying this I don't now, this timing is important isn't it?

"God I hope so," replied Iris.

"God bless," said Charlene expressing her admiration and genuine frioendship.

They stayed up for a couple of hours but smoked no more joints during which time Charlene disclosed that she wanted out of the drug circle altogether. A circle they had both been a part of, the people last night for example were bad news.

"I don't know how I'm going to do it."

"Step by step, maybe we need a hobby."

"Or a job."

"For you may be, but I can't see that happening for me, not now anyway."

"I will go with you tomorrow."

"Thank you Charlene you are a . . ." At which point she broke down in tears . . ."Sorry I don't know how it got to this . . . I was only . . . look I'm shaking." She offered her slender hand up for proof, it looked wet from tears fragile and vulnerable. At which point Charlene leaned over and hugged Iris tight in her arms. She withdrew her arms looked at Iris and said: "I must go now, go to bed and I will call tomorrow morning."

"Sorry Charlene I will be strong." At which point she took a breath and fanned her face with her left hand and said: "See you tomorrow."

Chapter 3

Surprisingly Iris was able to sleep without much trouble, though she looked up at the ceiling for a while, content just to be exhausted and comfortable. All her worries seemed to be vast enough to be somehow disassociated. There was nothing to be done she just had to sleep which that night came very naturally.

Waking up she seemed to have nothing to remember so she turned over before she realised where she was. God it was depressing, then her mind set was to score. Damn it she was angry with herself for the thought of wanting to use, momentarily though it was.

It was still early; a quarter past nine. Dragging herself out of bed she reached for a cigarette and a packet of rizla and . . . "Sod it" she said throwing the rizla on the floor and lit the cigarette.

With a cup of coffee and some cigarettes she set about watching morning television.

At a quarter to ten she was ready for bed again and so she lay down for a while.

At a quarter past ten there was a knock at the door and Charlene waited to be let in.

"Aghh . . ." Stammered Iris. This all felt very inconvenient and she banged the pillow with her fist, before realising how lucky she was to have friend like Charlene. She did not wish

I Won't Do Wrong

that she might sound ungrateful. So she turned her head and sobbed; "Coming" she shouted.

Charlene was there fully made up looking fabulous with her Afro Caribbean roots glowing she was a proud young woman with a heart of gold. This was Irises day and Charlene was going to make it work.

"You alright babe?" She said. Iris let her in "I'm in peaces but I'll do." Replied Iris. Charlene strode over to the window and drew back the curtains. Turned around and cleaned last nights plates and mugs, walked into the kitchen and put the kettle on. "Are you ready for it?" She shouted through to Iris.

"Yes . . . Yes." She answered holding her head in her hands.

By one thirty they were ready to head into town to the clinic. It was a nerve racking time for Iris but Charlene's strength brought them to the waiting room with ten minutes to spare. They both picked up a magazine from the pile of out dated issues on the table. Scouting through them though any constructive reading was impossible for Iris with so much on her mind. There was a lady a few years her senior sitting to her right, two young men in front of her Charlene to her left and a surprisingly attractive young man who seemed to command the atmosphere and required respect or at least attentiveness.

There was no delay and at one fifty nine and thirty seconds her name was called out. A minute is quite a long time she thought, well here anyway.

Charlene waited outside and only had to wait for ten minutes when Iris wondered out looking pleased holding a prescription of methadone in her hand.

"Well done babe." She said and took her arm for comfort, they walked out together and the world seemed so open for the both of them. It was like everything was at their feet a whole new start, they both felt it but it was still an eerie experience a new one, one to be cherished, if its meaning was as individual as their lives ahead, and a turning point that they have been allowed to share, a bond of friendship.

Two months later;

Iris was doing exceptionally well and was beginning to wean herself off the methadone. Herself and Charlene still lived up and down from each other at the flats and all the slum antics of drug abuse had gone. No more plumes of smoke drifting in the corridors and no more half cut people to climb over in the stair well. And had made more friends (in the other tenants, who were over the moon at the transformation of the building they lived in.)

Charlene was starting a new job at a laundrette it was not much fun but then most jobs aren't but if they are then that is more for the good as well.

If anything Iris was getting bored during the day but she had her meetings with other heroine users/ and ex-users. And being so young listening to the older addicts she realised just how dramatic the life change is, how it grabs hold of your mindset and constantly pulls you away from any comparable relationship with the world and the non-user.

She felt lucky and terrified very very scared and still the thought of scoring was out the window, which was brilliant, and strike two.

I Won't Do Wrong

Very recently Charlene had become aware of 'the bigger picture'. By which I mean that now her life was on an even keel her mind was naturally drifting into World issues. One thing that she could not fathom was whale hunting, made illegal in British waters in the seventies and eighties. Now Japan has been whale hunting legally even up to today. She loved what Green Peace were doing to sabotage the hunting. And then she saw something: Iceland!? Surely that must be wrong, I like Iceland she thought. How did the man describe it 'like the culling of cattle at a sustainable rate to help keep the population healthy. 'Uh hello', she thought.

Still she went on flicking though the magazine looking at various product advertisements and a column on Britney Spears. "Sing with passion shouldn't she" Charlene spoke aloud to her work colleague. "Who dear?" She was a bit older than Charlene, well a lot older.

"Britney Spears, do you remember her?"

"Oh yes."

"She should sing from her heart."

"Yes dear, is machine number two on?"

"All done."

"You can get along now if you want I'll finish up here."

"That has to be lifted to up there."

"Yes I'll do it."

"It will be my deed for the day." Charlene said with a smile.

When she got home she looked up Green Peace on the computer and typed in Iceland, probably one of the nicest places in the world. After she had drunk a glass of wine she went downstairs to see Iris.

They spoke for a while about all sorts but mainly the existence of anything worthwhile. Iris was feeling lonely and with nothing to do, at least nothing of external substance that she could get her teeth stuck into. Life was dull and they both claimed tired of their insular worlds. After all here are two intelligent good looking women with oodles of potential.

"What do you think of a holiday?" Asked Charlene.

"The chance but I'm tied down with the methadone and I have no money."

"Just a few days then."

"Yes definitely but I will need to seriously consider my finance."

"But you have more now that you are not using, I swear it wont be a fortune."

"Come on then what have you got planned?"

"Iceland. We can have those spring heated spas in the snow it will be fab."

"And the whales . . ."

"Yes, I want to see who they are and what they see."

"Then the answer is yes, we're going on holiday!"

They both were very excited at the prospect of seeing something other than the insides of their two worlds, the same ceilings, streets and the same monotony day in day out.

Charlene booked the tickets over the internet and found some cheap return journey flights for the day after tomorrow. Iris had enough methadone to last for the next week, she was due to pick up some more tomorrow which would fit perfect with their plans. She did tell the team that she was leaving for Iceland but that she would only be away for a short break of may be four or five days. "Be strong." one of them said.

'I don't think there will be much powder on the island.' Iris almost said, instead she saw reason, smiled and sort of waved her hand as she closed the door. For the first time in ages she was happy excited even and the smile broad across her face was proof.

Chapter 4

The plane took off and landed and although it seemed a little too much like a London bus it proved safe enough. They stepped of the stair well and embraced the cold Icelandic air.

Firstly they should hire a car for their stay, this was all done at the airport and they were soon on their way to the Bed and Breakfast that came with the package deal. Charlene was good at getting stuff and a diamond girl all round. She had managed to get the car half price if they stayed at the required address which happened to be on at half price also, something about refurbishment. All in all this holiday was sorted out for fifty pounds each, and they had Tuesday to Friday to do as they pleased.

Iris pleaded to get a drink at the local free house. They walked in through swinging doors, like those seen in western films, and half expected spurs, guns, hats and waist coats, and a bar tender drudging around pouring roughly measured whiskies into glass tumblers. But it was all very civilised. There was a group of young men drinking and being merry, their converse stopped for a moment while they checked out the new girls. One of them came over and put some money on the counter.

"Glass of wine each for the ladies please Bob."

I Won't Do Wrong

"Right you are son, don't go leading these girls astray . . . Watch him." He said and winked a good eye to show his opinion of their friendly nature.

They had a right laugh that night and although Charlene was worried that Iris might have been drinking too much, she was not her minder, and she too was getting flirty with all the strong lager on tap. Iris was enjoying her self which is just what the doctor ordered she kissed one of the men and promised to see him again. Charlene on the other hand had a more teasing of evenings with Dannie a man she liked . . . a lot.

The next morning Iris had more to worry about than what she had done the night before. She was feeling very low. Charlene had of course noticed this and promised that they would both benefit from the healing powers of the naturally heated spas. "Worry about things later." Charlene was adamant that what ever might happen they should have a good time. Dannie had offered to show them to the spa's and around the island. Iris was half dreading half hoping that Dannie would bring his mate Thomas was his name. It was not that she didn't like him, because she did, it was more that on an evening you can maintain a certain anonymity, and now she would have to show him all her luggage. She worried too much, she was beautiful and bright she had merely got caught in a very intricate, beautifully sewn but lethal web that is heroin. And any man worth his salt would understand and respect her motivation to be clean and therefore show compassion and judge her not on this negative aspect of her life's journey but on the person that she really was. After all what she was doing, and she was doing more than simply giving up heroin, she was shattering an iron grasp of the devil himself, and that is a marvel in every sense.

Danni and Tom turned up at about a quarter to eleven. Iris blushed which really caught Toms eye.

"Morning girls." Dannie said. "Your chariot awaits." He pointed across to a perfectly clean four by four. "This he said is Toms pride and joy, come on it'll be fun. Have you got bathing stuff?"

"Yes we thought we were going in our car."

"Tom and Dannie laughed at the age old citroen that although perfectly good was dwarfed by Toms adequately marvellous truck of a car.

"We will see more in this, come on." Dannie said.

Dannie ushered Charlene forward, leaving the slightly shy Tom and Iris to follow.

"Sober." Said Tom

"I know." Replied Iris who took his arm and made for the truck.

"First" Said Dannie, "We shall go and see the blow hole it erupts every thirty four minutes it is scolding hot so be wary, and then we shall bath in natures finest hot tub." He reached for the glove compartment and took out a selection of CD's of which he selected Johnny Cash.

"Put a dampener on things Dan," said Tom "Put Queen on." They settled with The Stereophonics.

"Good choice" Said Iris and with this the girls were both contented at the same time and were very pleased to be there.

It was only a short drive until they came across the blow hole. The glaciers were in the background and it was

I Won't Do Wrong

idyllic. Just to the rear of the hot pool (Geezer) that erupted periodically was a place to eat. They would get some food and watch the water. Iris had a lemonade and Charlene had a glass of white wine and the lads had a pint of bitter each.

"So what brought you to Iceland?" Asked Tom.

"It is such a beautiful place." Replied Iris.

"The monotony was brain numbing for us both."

"Iris was beginning to clam up. She knew that at the hot spa her arms would be exposed, and she knew that she would have to say something before that happened. And it was about to happen so it would have to be here in the café before they left. So she sat up straight and moved her attention to Tom.

"This is not an easy thing for me to do but I will be straight with you."

"Go on then I have thick skin."

"I'm on the methadone treatment."

Tom kept on a long gaze, his eyes telling Iris a story of a compassionate mind, finally he said; "How are you doing on it, I mean I don't know much about it. How long were you on it for?"

"About two years, a bit less."

"That's not too long I mean I know that your young but you will have done most of your growing up before you got caught up with the wrong people, which has got to be good."

"Your right it is and I'm not feeling like jeopardising my chance, I've gripped onto it and I'm not alone I have Charlene, she has always been straight and has been a tower of strength."

"Well I like your company and I'm glad you told me, we will have fun and I promise you these surroundings can cure anything."

"Thank you Tom you're a lovely man."

Chapter 5

When they reached the hot spa and the lads stripped down and put on some bathing shorts. It was all quite funny as the girls changed behind the car on one side and the men on the other and it was really cold.

"I've not been here for an age." Said Dan.

"Don't you look at us." Shouted across Charlene.

"Wear your trainers." Said Dan.

"These cost me a fortune." Stammered Iris.

"Yeah about ten years ago." Laughed Charlene.

"Last one in." Shouted Iris. Tom followed and grabbed her by the waist slowing her down. "Fall on this and you will be the last one in." The ice was thick on the ground supporting shards of dangerous rock. "Come on you can sit here if you like there is a natural ledge." Tom and Iris slowly immersed themselves and Tom, finding a rock below the surface to sit on, held on to Iris and the warmth and the companionship was strong and they were quiet for a time.

"Come on guys." Shouted Tom to Dannie and Charlene "Before the water gets cold."

Everyone laughed and Dannie with Charlene walked across being very close sharing some mental space. Charlene felt like she had met the most perfect man in the world. It was like destiny and feeling smooth and united they slowly sank into the water.

This was a sensual time for all of them, Iris could tell that Charlene was very fond of Dannie and she too felt at ease and passionate simply to be in Toms arms. She felt like a woman, like it should be (she thought), vulnerable but safe, powerful yet passive and warm.

This was truly bliss and despite everything the chance meeting of these four people could not have been better orchestrated, and there was a very strong sense of being in the presence of something huge, something compassionate and something great.

Charlene was looking gorgeous and Dannie knew he was on to something fab. He was perhaps a little over cautious but Charlene liked this. She realised at this point that they knew almost nothing of these two guys, and so decided to be asked into their lives and so asked what Dan did for a living.

"I work on the sea." Said Dan.

"You're a fisherman." Said Charlene.

"Of sorts." replied Dan.

All so soon Charlene's heart sank. She knew what this meant, though she couldn't bring herself to say it in words. But she tried.

"Do you catch big fish."

"You could say that." He replied.

"Do you know . . ." Said Charlene " . . . that we came over here for two reasons. One for the spa's and beauty and two because we could not understand how and why Iceland still supported Whaling, is that what you do?"

Tom looked at Dannie and said "It is an age old tradition and all the Whale is used in some manner."

I Won't Do Wrong

I thought that Japan does this but Iceland is such a civil place you know what I mean a kin."

The atmosphere had dropped and suddenly they were just four people in an uncomfortable position.

Dan knew that he had fallen in love and didn't care for Whaling when analysed by Charlene's theological position.

"Look, you like us yea, well people here are nice, and these guys, well there fathers and there fathers fathers and their forefathers fathers fathers have all done this and its all they know and when you get asked to go along the excitement of the sea well it is exciting. Can you understand?"

"You know I do." Spoke Charlene. "But now right here and now, do you live for it?"

"No I don't. It pays the bills and puts food on the table I can't do anything else."

"You know how to fish though."

"Yes I do."

"Well couldn't you do that instead."

"It's not very lucrative but I could do it. There is vast over fishing already but yes I could do and I could be happy doing so but poorer. I am the first to admit I love the sea and the danger and the excitement it has me hooked. I know that we've just met but if you stay then something inside me will have been restored, a pilot light that will make life a little easier and little better. Much better. In fact damn it I don't like whaling any more." Dan pronounced "The Whale I will not harm or promote the harming of" Dan voiced to the world and though no one else could hear the four of them knew it was meant. You represent a much wider world than I'm used to, but I want to be in this world. A world that you yourself personify. You must stay longer see if this life is what gets you."

Everyone had been quiet and still . . . just listening until Tom spoke;

"I agree with everything that Dan has said we will be poorer but we will still have the sea. There is a chance of tourism people love whales. It's a fact. So we will show them whales and if the money is in it then that will decide, I hope you are right."

Iris stepped in and said "Money is only fantastic when it is well earned you may have all the piles of cash in the world but happiness comes with reward and that can not be bought."

"I know I earn my money but I like it, and I'm not embarrassed to say that I like material things. But when I put up to be counted what is lost and what is gained I can not say that the scales are in my favour and that I don't like. I like whales, your right they are majestic and we should try another tack, we should invest in tourism instead. People like you will come and holiday and spend their money. We have a healthy population and we should keep it that way so that there are more to show the tourist and maybe more would follow suit may be even Japan. The ball has to start rolling from somewhere and if it is rolling past us now then we must add to its bulk and send it on its way mission accomplished, hunting stopped tourism started."

"I like that." Commended Iris.

"It's all about advertising." Said Charlene. "You tell the right people and they will visit guaranteed. They will flock here, we did."

"I think you are right." Said Dan, for closure, and looked at Tom.

"You English You're a bit crazy, but I think you are right as well."

"Good." said Charlene "Have you ever been to England?"

"No" Said Tom.

"No" Said Dan

"You must come it is a very interesting place." Said Charlene.

Both Tom and Dan stayed quiet trying to work out if this was an invite or a statement of intellect.

"That's settled then you will come back with us and stay for a while, see what you think of the big city, you will have fun and then you can come back and do what you do here, its up to you, are you romantic enough?"

This approach confused Tom, Dan and Charlene for a while and then Tom started chuckling and said "I am surely the luckiest man, my head is in a spin but I really want to go."

"Done and dusted then." Said Iris.

"I guess so" said Charlene quietly, a little embarrassed.

"Come on lets get something to eat." Suggested Dan.

A little of the spontaneous was a bit spicy but the air was calm and there were still the sparks of love especially between Charlene and Dan, but Iris and Tom were not far behind.

Chapter 6

They went back to the village where both Tom and Dannie had been born and educated. It was a small fishing community. The sort of place where everyone knew everyone and where two beautiful women stood out, especially on the arms of these local lads.

They were taking the girls to a seaside restaurant that served fresh seafood some of it still alive.

Iris ordered octopus, she was sure that she would not like it but it was exciting and here horizons were as broad as they had ever been.

Tom found this a bit confusing; save the whale but eat the octopus? He let it go though. Iris too was a bit confused she didn't know why but she thought that ordering this was ok probably because she almost knew that she wouldn't like it. Double whammy. But then she was hungry. All this thought was a bit ahead of her though she might like it and why not? She couldn't answer that.

Charlene ordered Sea Bass partly because it was the only one she recognised save the cod and mackerel and she had never had it before, well she was on holiday and she had never tried it before.

"It doesn't get fresher than this." Said Dan.

As predicted the octopus was chewy and far too alien for her, too primal, which served her right in many respects for she had chosen it for what it was even though she could tell that she wouldn't like it. Leave the octopus to roam the seas not the seaside restaurants, was her obvious conclusion. There was whale on the menu and the owner was pleased to say that they had caught one just yesterday. The men would normally have ordered whale but in the presence of the girls opted for Halibut a fish that goes with any occasion, a safe bet. But with Iris eating octopus perhaps they shouldn't have bothered.

Half way through the meal Iris put down here knife and fork and said; "It's beat me I don't like it."

Tom waved a hand to Moraine "Cod and chips for the lady please."

"The octopus beat you." She asked Iris.

"Yup I don't think I should eat things like this. She raised a hand to her mouth and ran to the toilet. If only she knew where it was, running in circles she found the door, exited and leaned over the sea barrier to let loose the content of her stomach.

She had only taken her methadone just prior to entering the restaurant and the thought of the slimy octopus proved incompatible.

Apologising as she came in she sat back at the table.

"Its the methadone I'm so embarrassed."

"No no eat what you want, you might find this food more palatable."

He was right and although Iris was shaking a bit and eating very slowly, she seemed consciously content and happy just to sit there.

"How are you doing with the program?" Tom asked sympathetically.

"Its been nine weeks now, I want to get off the methadone as well."

"That is a brilliant thing." Said Tom.

"At the moment I just want to stay here, I think home, if I can call my flat home is a very depressing place."

"You know that I still want to go back with you?" Tom said raising his voice to be heard. "I think that you are mad and kind, I think you are magnificent." He said and leaned across and hugged her with affection.

Dan looked across at Charlene for he wanted her to stay in Iceland. It was all to perfect which unnerved him slightly still he went with it and said; "Will you stay for a while, here in Iceland, I have so much more to show you?"

"Yes I will you are lovely." She gave him her puppy eyes and Dan melted.

Chapter 7

The plane was scheduled for three fifteen the next day and Tom had managed to change the name on Charlene's boarding card at an extortionate rate, something Tom could not get his head around but there it is. Charlene was staying for a while. There was something about this whole experience that adorned, in her mind, space that was new and warm. A place that perhaps she always wanted to find. It was a little eerie but brilliant, it had all been so impulsive and sudden but she wasn't going to let it go for an instant, not until it betrayed her at least, things always seemed to betray her but would Dan and Iceland?

She waved goodbye to Iris and Tom and then there were two. They hugged for a while and then made for the exit and went to the local watering hole. The log fire was ablaze they sat drinking coffee and it was just perfect.

Two months later:

Iris and Tom were now living together somewhere in Vauxhall they had bought a dog a Labrador cross Collie. It was the most adorable thing and brought them closer together. Iris was off the methadone program and was a real success, her dark flat was now a distant memory and she made her living from a job at the local bar. This at least would tide her over and it was fun. If she needed a change she felt capable now, but at the moment life was too good to worry.

Tom was not out of his depth in the city though he planned to move more rural when the time was right. He didn't really know what to do, all this was a long way from fishing. A friend of his father had given him an opportunity to train in butchery which he decided to accept. He picked it up very quickly, he was good at it. He felt like the wealthiest person in all of Britain. For once he was able to sort of visualise a future, with Iris, and a life that he never really thought he would ever achieve. Charlene had loved living in Iceland and had of course moved in with Dannie. He had the most honest and quaint place to live. Very thick stone walls to keep the heat in and to protect them from the fierce weather they sometimes encounter in Iceland. She wished to get a job right away and did so. Dannie no longer worked for the whalers, who too were losing the battle of public support. No he was a hand on a fishing boat so was out at sea for lengthy stints. It was for this reason as well that she needed a job, to do something with her time, for the money and for purpose. The man at the post office was a kind sort and his aid for the past thirty years was due to retire, and to be honest had been for a number of years already. Still he invited Charlene to help out and learn the ropes. She really wished for this to be the rest of her life or at least for a long while.

Of course the couples met up frequently but mainly when Tom was home visiting his family who lived in the next village. They would meet up to have something to eat and a jar of Iceland's finest bitter.

What happens next is in our hearts.

Acknowledgement

This tale is one that is of the most fortunate in nature. Cold turkey, the physical response to coping without a drug can be crippling and is about as tough as it gets. And so I am in no way scoring this addiction with flippancy. But this story is possible and I am writing with the aim and hope that the process of withdrawal from addiction may be taken on with optimism and that individuals may be inspired at least a little bit to awaken and see the dawn of a new day every day with the emotion that hope springs eternal.

Kusassi

This tale is of a baby Orang-Utan born in the breaches of Borneo and is based on the life of one Kusassi a male who ran away from the rescue camp. Firstly however I will try to explain the uncompromising and impossible position of the native Borneo Orang-Utan. And as is oh so common. Oil is at the forefront, not crude oil but palm oil. This is cropped using the palm oil tree and is responsible for a huge percentage of vegetable oil that you may find in any store in foods ranging right the way through the spectrum. There is an almost unlimited demand for this oil and where there is money there is also greed. In fact it is not only the wild life that is being lost and put in danger but also a local population of local tribesmen. But at the moment I shall focus on a particular Orang-Utan Kusassi who went missing and then was found. (My story is one that explains Kusassi's life growing up on his own without his mother (which is nigh on impossible). Of course I have no idea how he managed but it could have been a bit like this:

Bless him he was one of many baby Orang-Utan's saved from the claws of the unjust struggle. His mother had been killed in the clearings and he was captured for the pet trade in China. This is where he would still be if it were not for an undercover team that found him and brought him back to the wilds of Borneo. He however could not be let into the wild as he would have died. For there is little or no food available for a juvenile Orang-Utan who doesn't know where to look. No it would normally stay by his mothers side for three or four years learning what there is to eat how to get it and when each food sort is in season. So he remained at the sanctuary with many others, a sanctuary that had been set up for orphan and injured Orang-Utan's, run by the most formidable and fabulous woman whom for her dedication I adore.

There was however a sad day when the keepers at the rescue centre realised that he was no longer there. They called and searched high and low (aptly of course for a monkey) but he was lost and only a toddler. His chances of survival were just about zero. He was one and a half to two years old and should rightly be hugging onto his mother for another year. Now what happened next is the story of one truly magnificent animal. It is a story of how he might have survived, how he actually did so is and will remain unknown.

As unseen by the keepers at the sanctuary Kusassi had noticed a stray male in the undergrowth and had gone to explore. His view of the humans was low not only because they had killed his mother but also because of his mistreatment, as a caged pet in the Chinese market, where he was kept.

This time he was free and he followed the scent of the male he had seen but was soon he was lost in the jungle. Now this sanctuary was in a part of Borneo that was considered a reserve, not that large, and for his survival he must cross the plantations to a place further north. All he knew was that this male was his key to survival, he would unsurreptitiously show him what foods to eat and when and where they were available. Kusassi was stalking him and he needed too, the

I Won't Do Wrong

large male knew but did not let on. They had come to a clearing with almost nowhere to hide. Kusassi watched him look toward the mountain to his left and then to the sun on his left and took a step into the plantation. They walked, Kusassi eight steps adrift, this was as close as the adult male would allow him which appeared suitable for both, for their struggle was of survival not of joy or companionship, at this point.

As sudden as the start of a tropical down pour and from out of nowhere came the sound of a vehicle. A shot was fired narrowly missing Kusassi. It would appear as though they had not seen Henry, his soon to be guardian Orang-Utan, who leapt up at the open aired four by four. He was mad but didn't know what to do so he reached for the keys and grabbed the gun before running off. Kusassi followed him and from thereon they were bonded and the adult male took him under his wing. It didn't feel natural to him but it was right and that's all he knew.

The next few months were to be critical for his survival and he was quite literally knocking on heavens door for almost every day in the first three months.

Henry was a real survivor he was tough as well as gentle. His own bit of jungle was on the other side of the plantation and they went at a fair pace to get there. There was fruit a plenty but as Kusassi was later to understand this territory was once twice the size and he had seen first hand how his family had been all but wiped out. Of course the male is a loner only having brief contact with the group of females and young, but his eyes had seen everything. The thought of Henry offering Kusassi to his female group did not occur to him, the bond that they had created was different somehow, more matter of fact.

So he had found himself kin of kinds, it was a bit lonely but the memory of his days in a small cage, and the fact that he was here once again in the jungle, put a smile on his face as Gods smile was surely looking down on him, and this chap Henry really was ok.

Henry was a keen guardian, though this sweet little Orang-Utan pushed his curiosity to limits he never knew he had. One time Kusassi stopped moving after a fair few hours Henry became concerned, he walked over and stood over him and gently pocked him. They were near a stream so he went over took a great big leaf and spooled some water into it's curled base. He gently poured the water onto Kusassi's lips and almost immediately he was revived. He then chewed up some figs and passed the mush into Kusassi's mouth, and after more water he could once again be left to follow, though he went no where far until Kusassi was looking much better.

He was with Henry for close on two years and at times he had to fend for himself much more out of survival than some sort of guided education, it made him tough and wise beyond his years. He had seen the group of females from time to time but had never ventured too close, not yet, he would always think. Henry of course had to perform for the continuation of the line, in breeding season, but he would always find young Kusassi if he ran off scared. He was after all Kusassi's only constant and Henry had become used to him, he was simply a part of his integral life and would feel a great sense of loss had Kusassi died or wondered off lost.

This bond although strong was not a naturally generic relationship and it took all of Kusassi's early effort to maintain Henry's acceptance. He did so despite the natural law of things and probably because of them as well, for he had a real loathing of humans (If that is an Orang-Utan can feel such hate I think they are too sweet for hate or jealousy or resentment I just don't think it is in their make up which is why it is up to us to save and help them).

There were times when Kusassi, with no one to play with, got into pickles. His first attempt at crossing the river that ran through Henry's territory was a close shave. He did not understand the forces involved and got swept away. Henry was on his feet immediately running and swinging and jumping for half a kilometre through the undergrowth on the river bank before wading in to save his little Orang-Utan friend.

Well Kusassi was four years old and Henry thought it right to usher him into the females, it was time, they would accept him now, or at least tolerate him because he always did deserve better. He made his first step into the camp, he was not sure, turning around he could not see Henry. At this point he nearly turned and ran but before he could do so he was already within the group with the Alfa female sniffing at him. Without much hesitation she started to groom him gently going through his hair picking out any untoward ticks and flies and leaf.

This was a sign to the others as well as Kusassi of his acceptance. It was all a bit too much and after an hour or so he felt overwhelmed and wanted to go back to his solitude and ever so lonely tranquillity he was used to it was a melancholic life but it was all he knew and he liked it. So he was in two minds, he went around all the regular fruit trees but could not find Henry anywhere. Left with the options of staying alone in the quiet coolness of the jungle or go back to the family that had just accepted him as part of the group was difficult. Then he remembered what Henry had told him once: 'Take a chance and grab hold of it, you will know when' At this point those words seemed very apt, perhaps he had said this because he knew that one day he would not be able to look after him, in effect pre-empting this occasion.

Well Kusassi was thinking that a bit of both would be nice, but if he left he knew that he would probably never find Henry and may even be left with no one which in the present situation could be fatal in his journey through the Jungle. He still did not have the knowledge to survive there were too many plantations, which although growing they offered almost nothing to jungle life except general infertility. So it was either one or the other, and he chose not the easiest path but the best one, that being the family of course.

Before long he was five years old and no longer needed the closeness that he had been deprived of his whole life and that Henry had done his best to offer. It was strange to see how little there was to worry about and how mentally underdeveloped his contemporaries were. He had more fun wrestling with the adolescent monkeys he was cheeky but well tolerated.

Gladly from here his life changed and he loved it, he had time to mess around to work out family life and he could teach his contemporise the law of the jungle as he had seen it.

It was only two years later that he decided to go and visit the camp that he had run away from all that time ago. He was no longer dependant and he once again walked in the Jungle as himself and by himself as adult males do. He needed nothing now and that is why he felt he could go back. And he did and he was the Alfa male everywhere he went for the next fifteen years he answered to no one and was magnanimous brilliant and handsome, quite the architectural ape.

Kusassi has had a miraculous escape but the truth remains very bleak for Orang-Utan's and many more animals and well I suppose it is up to the politicians to do some thing because we owe it to our children as well as to nature. Every generation deserves to leave a good legacy otherwise there seems no point and I hope that this one may be ours.

The Length of a Wing
Chapter One

Resigned to the hum of the wind Percy looked across the water that was his destination to meet his friends only to find no one else there. He had been a bit behind schedule so his expectation, reasonably enough, was to find George, Sophie, Ken and the rest of the gang already arrived and swimming around the lake, as they had planned to do so this morning but they were not there. He checked the water which was nice and warm to the touch and as he got in he decided yes this is warmer we could stay here for a while. But he had to admit that this lake was not so familiar, in fact he didn't recognise it at all.

"Right at the castle, so perfectly situated, over and through the lake district stopping of for a pint on the way at the pond in the stone walled village, straight down the M6 change and turn right at the M42 and follow the valley to the water." He thought. "Or was it left at the M42, I always forget that bit he chuckled to himself, for his memory was not good for these things.

To his right he notices a Heron tall and slender and very proud with a true heir of the English gentleman.

"What What." He said

"Have you seen any Swans?"

"I have seen many Swans, had a race with a charming Mute Swan only last month. You of course are of the whooper Swan variety. And you are altogether much smaller but may I say more beautiful. The prowess of the mute is stronger I'll grant you that. Oh yes far greater somewhat of the loner though I must say that is of their character. A fine example you are my friend."

"Yes yes thank you but I am looking for my friend George he would not say to be somewhere and then not to be so."

"You are young are you not? Is this your first migration, because if it is then your team leader should never have left you on your own, it is unreasonable, were you lazy or was it something more sociable?"

"I am my own boss."

"Yes I am sure that you are but that was not my question were you ostracized."

"As sure as I found my way here I wasn't."

"Yes but you are in the wrong place, are you not. Which leads me to think only one thing, that you were considered a bird beyond your years. Yes indeed it is a fine thing to be regarded as competent even if only in a matter of fact manner. Yes yes tell me where you are going and how many were in your circled group."

"There are forty two." answered Percy

"Do you know I think I can take you to where they will be. Yes yes I know where thy will be. They will be missing you I shouldn't wonder if a scout will find us first, still how are you for flight?"

"Well I am very good but I will rest up here tonight and eat upon the cordon vert."

"I see now why they assembled respect on your abilities, some what of a genius. What."

"I don't know if I am that but French I like. There was a gull in Iceland he was French and I learnt a lot from him.

He promised to show me the nature of France I am to fly there after my eighth week at Walreston Water."

"That is where I believed them to be. It is not far. We shall leave tomorrow. I can see that you are a very capable Swan."

They drifted apart from each other to do some serious eating when Percy realised that he had not asked for his name. "General." he called "What is your name"

"My name . . ." He said " . . . is Earnest"

They both sloped off to eat but mainly to rest. Earnest being a Heron was always immaculately kept, mysterious and solitary. The air around him was his castle as he was at the very top of all things around. Even the Humans did not encroach upon his day to day living.

Chapter two

They slept well with only the cry of an owl and the barking of a dog some distance away breaking the tranquillity of the night.

When morning broke Percy noticed the Canada geese, "Surely" he thought " . . . these birds were not here yesterday."

There was a question in his voice and although he was simply talking to himself there came a reply from behind him; "If they were then I would not be hungry today!"

Percy had no time to turn around. So flapping his wings he began to raise from the waters edge, but alas he was not quick enough. He knew all to well what this meant, which was dinner, he himself was going to be dinner. He had heard of foxes it was one of the first thing that you are taught in nursery. The old and wise would recollect stories of fallen friends.

As it happened on this occasion Percy got away, though the fox had clamped its jaws on his left wing which was now hanging in an uncomfortable and painful manner.

Earnest had heard the commotion and had come straight over to see if there was anything he could do.

"Can you make it to the pontoon?" He asked. "It is safe to rest there."

After they had reached the pontoon Ernest had a good look at the wing. "It is broken in two places my friend"

I Won't Do Wrong

"How am I to fly with a bad wing?"

"The answer to that is that you are not. I have seen this before and if you are prepared to stay still for six weeks then you may fly. They are not as bad as I have seen. They are not compound and they are aligned. You must stay here while I talk to the committee, I will favour your case and I have as you have seen some influence in the committee. But for now you must rest."

Some animals were easier to listen to than others. The Canada geese for example tended to natter to each other in a manner more associated to madness than to any respected order. But Ernest was somehow capable of transcending this barrier and installed a collective agreement which allowed them to act together for a single purpose. Which was quite a talent. And before long he had the geese bring food to Percy. Their long necks (although not as long as Percy's) were capable of fetching the freshest green weed and there was a plentiful supply.

Percy had never been still for any length of time before and well fed he was but well fed up he was also. He knew that there was no way he could refrain from movement. And when no one was looking he took a dip in the water, he had been marooned on the pontoon for four days. He had been warned though that the wing must remain straight and he was in the water and out again before anyone noticed and felt happy and clever. Though he had no reason to feel clever as Ernest had pre empted this notion and sat at a distance keeping an eye on his antics with an admiring smile.

During Percy's immobility Ernst had arranged to fly to Walreston Water. When he arrived it was clear that they thought he had gone the same way many do, a few each year.

"He is alive!" One of the elders shouted across to George and Sophie who were quite an item by this time.

Ken was there in a flash, asking all the questions he wanted answering at the same time.

"Calm down he is alright, if you want you can come with me and see him."

"Can I"

"It is up to you, you are a wild animal and so if it is in your nature to go, then you must do so." Said his mother.

So off they flew chatting on the way about Percy's trip to France and whether Ken was going with him. He said he wanted too and was aware of Percy's ambitious nature and that he wasn't surprised that he had got into trouble with the fox. He said this knowing well enough that if it were any one of them they would not have been so lucky. There was something about him that allowed him to deny injury and death, something that they could not put into words, but they all hoped that may be this incident would teach him of his mortality and curb his sometimes over energised enthusiasm, but he doubted it.

They arrived to find Percy floating in the middle of the lake, very gingerly, but with a certain air of honour, a hero he was. The ducks seemed to think so, they were surrounding him expressing admiration through line repetition. "Ducks are funny things." thought Ernest. Their behaviour is quite unique, they argue and squabble readily over the topic of interest and suddenly they will all agree and rant on about it for ages, but there was something very military and organised about it which had to be admired.

I Won't Do Wrong

Well they decided quite rightly so that Percy was quite something and were giving him the full army salute for as long as it took for the sun to fall.

They skidded back onto the lake. Ken a little more gracefully than Ernest some may say but as a Heron Ernest's grace was in the air still they were quite compatible friends.

Percy was mad to see Ken. Ernest had done him proud, he must remember though that his wing was still setting he curbed his excitement with the first strong shard of pain hit him.

"Enough of that." Cut in Ernest. "Do you want to fly again or not? Come now set up roost on the pontoon. It is still early days. Ken don't cause him movement."

They slept well that night but not until Percy had gone through his journey and found where he had gone wrong. It was the second bridge. It wasn't there last season and though they are taught to find that the brief is vulnerable to landscape change, he had not heeded this warning, he was too literal. But it was an easy mistake to make and he consoled himself so.

Chapter Three

When they awoke the whole flock had come to join them, which was a surprise but it seemed to take something from Percy's esteem it didn't seem like an adventure any more and he almost wished them gone. His emotions were high of course and it seemed like he had failed, but as one of the senior Swans pointed out to him—it was not a failure, more a turn of his tricks, as it was he who had brought them all there and it was he that would sail on without them later, leaving them to be reunited at a later date.

"This is family life I suppose and I will always be a part of it. Is that what you mean?" Asked Percy.

"Exactly, exactly so." Answered the elder.

The Moorhens and the Coots were feeling a bit guilty for what happened to Percy, especially Freddie who had been on watch. It was after all their responsibility to guard the reeds and banks at night. This was not an orderly responsibility but instinct, quite simply what they were good at, and although no one looked at them accusingly

Freddie felt vast disappointment. All those hours on guard with not so much as a strong wind and he closed his eyes for just one second, well he was just pleased no one had died.

It was a pied wagtail that noticed Freddie's slight depression, as it was his job to do so. Wagtails are as sharp as scissors they have the capacity to root out problems using cognitive processes. The Reed Warblers were also good at this but they were more into law than any other and able to judge happening. They were a bit fragmented but very capable and they judged no one to be at fault. Which helped heal Freddie's sorrow but consoled him to be more careful in future.

The flock decided to stay at Percy's side and there was even talk of coming back the next year. The food was plentiful and there was a really charming sense of the sunset and of tranquillity.

Chapter Four

With four weeks past Percy was feeling very down, he was a Swan with bucket loads of energy and with no vent, he was he felt, going to go mad. His wing was stronger and thanks to Edward (a lone Dove) the pain had died down. However this was mostly due to him taking pain relief leaves supplied by Edward who happened on the lake by chance. It was no chance however that he flew the length of Britain for this medicine. Doves are like this, so would pigeons be if they had not a slightly unhealthy relationship with the Humans, they always get so side tracked and never quite manage to finish any thing. They can however speak in sentences, but are always asking questions and not listening for an answer.

Ernest had called in a favour from an old friend he once knew from a lake the other side of Wales called Jim. He was a Peregrine Falcon and a very accomplished gymnast. Ernest had found Jim after some search in Snowdonia. He was not as young as he used to be and after some deliberation with the wife, who was incubating three eggs, allowed him to go, but only after he had stock piled food so that she would not have to leave the nest and run the risk of the cold on the eggs.

On the way to Ernest's lake Jim was preparing a plan of action. He said that although the break may heal in the six weeks his wing may still not be strong enough for flight. And that the earlier he could teach the physiotherapy required the sooner and better his recovery would be and the sooner he would be airborne.

Ernest did not explain to Jim that Percy was planning on flying to France in three weeks time, he would leave that until a glimmer of hope was exposed, if indeed it would be.

They arrived back at the lake and Jim was introduced to Percy and he had an examination of his injury.

"Hum . . . partial fracture of the upper tensile meticasle bone." He muttered. "Four weeks in . . . I should say that your chances are good and that you should start on a course of physiotherapy right away."

He went through some exercises with Percy, who was ecstatic with the newly found freedom of movement.

Jim got the Greater Tufted Grebe to right it down by laying weed on the flat surface of the pontoon, as was their intrinsic strength to do so.

'Stretch out wing to full expanse (slowly) circle twice to the left and twice to the right.' That would hurt enough to start with, thought Jim. "I want you to do these exercises as often as you can but no more that two or three times in the hour. I will be back in Five days time but for now I must leave. I have a wife and she will be missing me. Ernest thanked him and watched him fly over the tree line.

"Well." Said Ernest. "It is all looking quite good."

"Yes indeed I am so happy to move again I can't thank you enough. I feel like I could almost fly."

"Almost but you must not try because if you do then it may be that it will impair you permanently, be good and you, I promise, will flying again."

"You're the governor." Said Percy confident that he could manage these conditions.

Chapter five

Four weeks later and Percy had been immobile for eight weeks, he was beginning to think that he would never make it to Paris to see his friend. He knew well enough that it was today that he would have been off to France to see French Swans and have the guided tour by Pierre his Sea Gull friend. Ernest also knew that today was the day, and although he had not mentioned or referred to it, he was in his own way trying to keep Percy's flight schedule. Percy was a player he knew that and he had gods youthful energy and with every webbed toe crossed he set out to see if he was ready.

"Good morning." Said Ernest with a glint in his eye. "How are you today?"

"I am well" Said Percy, he looked purposefully at the Heron and asked; "Am I ever to make it to France?"

"You will and you are nearly ready, do you feel nearly ready?"

"I do but I have not as yet flown anywhere or even lifted into the air."

"Then you must try today."

This was an important moment and everyone knew it. It was time and if he were to ever fly again then he must today run the water and be airborne.

"Here we go." He said. And made for the sky with his somewhat clumsy run up and frantic flapping of his wings he gradually lifted into the air. He was in flight and he didn't want to land again, circling the lake he swooped low and then he looked at the horizon and slowly beat his wings. He was heading south with no pain and no impairment and before long he realised that he was on his way to France.

Back at the lake there was talk of his ability "His first flight, after such a traumatic injury. Is he insane? This was not doubted and everyone liked him and were in some small awe of this spontaneous moment. There were shouts of "Go for it Peirce." and "Go get um." and "Bon voyage" and "Vi La Vi"

Percy felt alive again and he was pleased that he had left the lake sure enough his friends were there, and he loved them all, but he was once again as free as a bird can be.

Have a safe journey.